What is Music?

SonLight Education Ministry
United States of America

A Suggested Daily Schedule

(Adapt this schedule to your family needs.)

5:00 a.m.  Arise–Personal Worship

6:00 a.m. Family Worship and Bible Class–With Father

7:00 a.m. Breakfast

8:00 a.m. Practical Arts*–Domestic Activities
         Agriculture
         Industrial Arts
         (especially those related to
         the School Lessons)

10:00 a.m. School Lessons
(Take a break for some physical exercise
during this time slot.)

12:00 p.m. Dinner Preparations
(Health class could be included at this time
or a continued story.)

1:00 p.m. Dinner

2:00 p.m. Practical Arts* or Fine Arts
(Music and Crafts)
(especially those related to
the School Lessons)

5:00 p.m. Supper

6:00 p.m. Family Worship–Father
(Could do History Class)

7:00 p.m. Personal time with God–Bed Preparation

8:00 p.m. Bed

*Daily nature walk can be in morning or afternoon.

The Desire of All Nations

This book is a part of a curriculum that is built upon the life of Christ entitled, "The Desire of All Nations," for grades 2-8. Any of the books in this curriculum can be used by themselves or as an entire program.

INFORMATION ABOUT THE 2-8 GRADE PROGRAM

Multi-level

This program is written on a multi-level. That means that each booklet has material for grades 2-8. This is so the whole family in these grades may work from the same books. It is difficult for a busy mother to have 2 or more children and each have a different set of books. Remember, the Bible is written for all ages.

The Bible—the Primary Textbook

The books in this program are designed to teach the parent and the student how to learn academic subjects by using the Bible as a primary textbook.

The Desire of Ages

The Desire of Ages by Ellen G. White is used as a textbook to go with the Bible. This focuses on the early life of Christ, when He was a child. Children relate best to Christ as a child and youth.

Lesson Numbers

The big number in the top right corner on the cover of this book is the Lesson Number and corresponds with the chapter number in the book *The Desire of Ages*. For example, Lesson 1 in the school program will go along with chapter 1 in *The Desire of Ages*. Usually each family starts at the beginning with Lesson 1. Most children have not had a true Bible program, therefore they need the foundation built. If there is academic material that they have already covered, they do the Bible part and review then pass quickly on.

Seven Academic Subjects

There are seven academic subjects in this program—Health, Mathematics, Music, Science–Nature, History/Geography/Prophecy, Language, Voice–Speech.

Language Program

A good, solid language program is recommended to be used along with the SonLight materials.

The Riggs Institute has a multi-sensory teaching method that accommodates every child's unique learning style. Their program is called *Writing and Spelling Road to Reading and Thinking*. Order by calling (800) 200-4840 or visit www.riggsinst.org. (Disclaimer: SonLight does not endorse the reading books recommended in the Riggs' program.)

Another option which you might find more user friendly and is similar to the Riggs program but from a Christian perspective is *Spell to Write and Read* by Wanda Sanseri. To order, call Wanda Sanseri at (503) 654-2300 or visit https://www.bhibooks.net/swr.html

"God With Us"
Lesson 1 – Love

The following books are those you will need for this lesson.
All of these can be obtained from www.sonlighteducation.com

The Rainbow Covenant – Study the spiritual meaning of colors and make your own rainbow book.

Health
What is Health?

Math
What is Mathematics?

Music
What is Music?

Science/Nature
What is Nature?

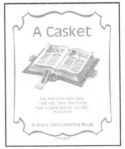

A Casket – Coloring book and story. Learn how to treat the gems of the Bible.

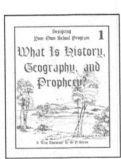

H/G/P
What is History, Geography and Prophecy?

Language
What is Language?

Speech/Voice
What is the Voice?

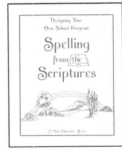

Spelling from the Scriptures

Bible Study – Learn how to study the Bible and helpful use tools.

Bible
The Desire of all Nations I
Teacher Study Guide

Student Study Guide

Bible Lesson Study Guide

Memory Verses
The Desire of all Nations I
Scripture Songs Book

and MP3 files

Our Nature Study Book – Your personal nature journal.

Outline of "The Desire of all Nations" Lesson 1

Bible	Health	Math	Music	Nature	H/G/P	Language	Voice

Week 1 | **Month 1**
Lesson 1

Day 1

Bible: Family Morning Worship *Covenant Notebook* (1) Music, MV Prayer, MV (2) Read pages 1-2 in the "Covenant Notebook" and discuss. (3) Sometime during the day take a nature walk looking for rainbows. (4) Begin finding pictures of complete rainbows to put into the plastic sheets behind the "Rainbows" page. Read and discuss the "Rainbows" page.

Health: Use these songs during this week, "All Things Bright & Beautiful," "This is My Father's World," and "We Shall Know." Find this music in *Christ in Song* book which is included in these materials under the title "Song Books."

READ THIS BEFORE BEGINNING

Cover the Teacher's Section of each school book before beginning that subject.

It is best to cover only a few concepts at once and understand them well and not run a marathon with a young person's mind. If this outline moves to fast for you SLOW down. Teach one idea and teach it well!

This school program is not a race with time, rather it is an experience with God. The parents are to represent their Father in Heaven before the children—students. Together learn about the Character Qualities and help one another in a godly manner to reach the finish line together.

INSTRUCTIONS

Day 2

Bible: (1) Music, MV Prayer, MV (2) Read page 3 in the "Covenant Notebook" and discuss. (Also use page 7)

Health: Lay out Lesson 1 of the School Program showing the the front covers of each book, *What is Health?, What is Mathematics?, What is Music?, What is Nature?,*

Math: *What is H/G/P?, What is Language?, and What is Voice?.* Each book will have a color cover of one of the colors of the rainbow. Place them in order as the rainbow colors

Music: deomonstrate in a picture. Refer to page 7 of the *Covenant Notebook* to see what each color means and how it relates to the subject that bears that color.

Nature: (Examples: Health = Christ sacrificed His body on the cross for you. Mathematics = Deals in numbers saved and lost.

H/G/P: Music = Right music can turn our thoughts from things of this world to Divinity. Nature = Right growth in character.

Language: H/G/P = The history of obedience and disobedience; geography of lands where the gospel is to be spread; prophecy telling us the future of those keeping the law.

Voice: Language and Voice = How God's royal people should write, speak, and act to prepare for His kingdom.

Bible	Health	Math	Music	Nature	H/G/P	Language	Voice
(3) Sometime during the day take a nature walk looking for rainbows. (4) Begin finding pictures of complete rainbows to put into the plastic sheets behind the "Rainbows" page. Read and discuss the "Rainbows" page. **Day 3-4** (1) Music, Prayer, MV (2) Read pages 4-9 in the "Covenant Notebook" and discuss. (3) Sometime during the day take a nature walk looking for white items (or the color pages). (4) Begin finding pictures of white things in nature to put into the plastic sheets behind the "White" page. Read and discuss the "White" page. **Day 5** Review what you have learned.							

INSTRUCTIONS

Once the white page is completed then move on to the red page and so forth, always finding things from nature for your pictures. And on your nature walks take the color you are currently working on. Do not look for man made things! Before going on the nature walk each day, read and discuss the information in the color section.

After day 5, and reviewing only what you have learned to that point, plan only to work on the *Covenant Notebook* one day a week until that book is finished (Use time in the afternoon and not during the regular school hours). However, do not forget to review the *Covenant Notebook* when you deem it necessary, and if you should find a new picture for it, stop and put it into *Covenant Notebook*. It gives you an opportunity to review lessons with the children.

Lesson 12 of Nature in this series is about the rainbow and would be a wonderful time to make a recommitment to God.

This *Covenant Notebook* is to prepare you for the 2-8 School Lessons. On week 2 begin the School Lessons.

Bible	Health	Math	Music	Nature	H/G/P	Language	Voice
Week 2 Lesson 1		START THE 2-8 PROGRAM, "The Desire Of All Nations."					
Day 1 "God With Us" (1) Music ("O Come, O come, Immanuel," "I Love Thee," "Thou didst Leave Thy Throne"), Prayer, MV (Mt 1:21) (2) Read and discuss Ge 3:14-15; 12:1-3. Discuss the Character Quality.	Day 1 *What Is Health?* (1) Open Bibles and read II Sa 20:9. (2) Read or tell information. Do pages 1-17 or what you can cover. Discuss.	Day 1 *What Is Math...?* (1) Open Bibles and read Mt 11:29. (2) Read or tell information. Do pages 1-8 or what you can cover. Discuss.				Day 1 *Writing and Spelling Road to Reading and Thinking (WSRRT)* (1) Do your daily assignments for *WSRRT.* If you are still working on this program continue until you finish at least the 2nd teacher's notebook.	

INSTRUCTIONS

If you are still using the *Family Bible Lessons* do them for one of your worships each day and use *The Desire of all Nations* for the other worship each day.

These are the items you will need for worship for *The Desire of all Nations* Bible program: Old King James Bible (NOT the New King James Bible)
"*The Desire of all Nations,*" Volume 1, Study Guide for the KJV Bible Lessons
The Desire of all Nations Teacher and Student Study Guides #1
(Chapters from *The Desire of Ages* Bible text book)
The Desire of all Nations Song Book #1 and CD Music #1
for Memory Verses
Christ in Song Song Book #1, 2, 3, 4

These are the items you will need for class time:

What is Health?; *What is Mathematics?*; *What is Music?*;
What is Nature?; *What is H/G/P?*; *What is Language?*; *and
What is Voice?*.
Our Nature Study Book   "The Casket" Story & Coloring Book
Bible Study
Road Map and Route Catalogue

Voice	Language	H/G/P	Nature	Music	Math	Health	Bible
	Day 2 *Writing and Spelling Road to Reading and Thinking* (1) Do your daily assignments for *WSRRT*.				**Day 2** *What Is Math...?* (1) Open Bibles and read Luke 6:38; Is 40:12; Ps 147:4; Is 40:26; Job 28:25. (2) Read or tell information. Do pages 9-22 or what you can cover. Discuss. **END**	**Day 2** *What Is Health?* (1) Open Bibles and read I Co 12:23. (2) Read or tell information. Do pages 18-26 or what you can cover. Discuss.	**Day 2** "God With Us" (1) Music ("O Come, O come, Immanuel," "I Love Thee," "Thou didst Leave Thy Throne"), Prayer, MV (Mt 1:21; Jn 8:28) (2) Read and discuss Gal 3:16; Ge 49:10; De 18:17-19; II Sam 7:12-17.
	Day 3 *Writing and Spelling Road to Reading and Thinking* (1) Do your daily assignments for *WSRRT*.			**Day 3** *What Is Music?* (1) Open Bibles and read Zeph 3:17. (2) Read or tell information. Do pages 1-6 or what you can cover. Discuss.		**Day 3** *What Is Health?* (1) Open Bibles and read Pr 26:2. (2) Read or tell information. Do pages 27-35 or what you can cover. Discuss.	**Day 3** "God With Us" (1) Music, Prayer, MV (Mt 1:21; Jn 8:28) (2) Read and discuss Ez 21:25-27; Lu 1:32; Isa 9:6-7.
	Day 4 *Writing and Spelling Road to Reading and Thinking* (1) Do your daily assignments for *WSRRT*.			**Day 4** *What Is Music?* (1) Open Bibles and read Re 14:2-3. (2) Read or tell information. Do pages 7-17 or what you can cover. Discuss.	**Day 4** *What Is Math...?* (1) Review.	**Day 4** *What Is Health?* (1) Review pages 1-35.	**Day 4** "God With Us" (1) Review what you have already covered.
	Day 5 Review			**Day 5**	**Day 5**	**Day 5**	**Day 5**

Find practical applications from your textbooks you have thus far used this week. You will find them listed under "**Reinforce**." Choose and use today.

Bible	Health	Math	Music	Nature	H/G/P	Language	Voice
Week 3 **Lesson 1** **Day 1** "God With Us" (1) Music, Prayer, MV (Mt 1:21; Jn 8:28) (2) Read and discuss Ps 45:1-8; 72:1-11; Is 53. **Day 2** "God With Us" (1) Music, Prayer, MV (Mt 1:21; Jn 8:28; Jn 8:50) (2) Read and discuss Zec 12:10; Jn 14:9; Mt 1:23; Jn 1:1-4. **Day 3** "God With Us" (1) Music, Prayer, MV (Mt 1:21; Jn 8:28; Jn 8:50; Phil 2:5-11) (2) Read and discuss *The Desire of Ages* 19-20:0.	**Day 1** *What Is Health?* (1) Open Bibles and read James 5:14. (2) Read or tell information. Do pages 36-39 or what you can cover. Discuss. **Day 2** *What Is Health?* (1) Open Bibles and read De 34:7. (2) Read or tell information. Do pages 40-44 or what you can cover. Discuss. **Day 3** *What Is Health?* (1) Open Bibles and read Ez 33:11. (2) Read or tell information. Do pages 45-53 or what you can cover. Discuss.		**Day 1** *What Is Music?* (1) Open Bibles and read I Ki 19:12. (2) Read or tell information. Do pages 18-30 or what you can cover. Discuss. **Day 2** *What Is Music?* (1) Open Bibles and read I Chr 13:8. (2) Read or tell information. Do pages 31-52 or what you can cover. Discuss. **END**	**Day 3** *What Is Nature?* (1) Open Bibles and read Ro 13:10. (2) Read or tell information. Do pages 1-11 or what you can cover. Discuss.		**Day 1** *Writing and Spelling Road to Reading and Thinking* (1) Do your daily assignments for *WSRRT*. **Day 2** *Writing and Spelling Road to Reading and Thinking* (1) Do your daily assignments for *WSRRT*. **Day 3** *Writing and Spelling Road to Reading and Thinking* (1) Do your daily assignments for *WSRRT*.	

Bible	Health	Math	Music	Nature	H/G/P	Language	Voice
Day 4 "God With Us" (1) Music, Prayer, MV (Mt 1:21; Jn 8:28; Jn 8:50; Phil 2:5-11) (2) Read and discuss *The Desire of Ages* 20:2-21:0.	**Day 4** *What Is Health?* (1) Open Bibles and read De 7:15; De 32:46; and Pr 4:20, 22. (2) Read or tell information. Do pages 54-60 or what you can cover. Discuss.			**Day 4** *What Is Nature?* (1) Open Bibles and read Ps 40:5; Ps 111:4. (2) Read or tell information. Do pages 12-17 or what you can cover. Discuss.		**Day 4** *Writing and Spelling Road to Reading and Thinking* (1) Do your daily assignments for *WSRRT*.	
Day 5 "God With Us" (1) Review.	**Day 5** *What Is Health?* (1) Review pages 1-60.	**Day 5** *What Is Math...?* (1) Review.	**Day 5** *What Is Music?* (1) Review.	**Day 5** *What Is Nature?* (1) Review pages 1-17.		**Day 5** *Writing and Spelling Road to Reading and Thinking* (1) Do your daily assignments for *WSRRT*.	
Week 4 Lesson 1							
Day 1 "God With Us" (1) Music, Prayer, MV (Mt 1:21; Jn 8:28; Jn 8:50; Phil 2:5-11) (2) Read and discuss *The Desire of Ages* 21:1-2.	**Day 1** *What Is Health?* (1) Open Bibles and read De 7:15; De 32:46; and Pr 4:20, 22. (2) Read the story. Do pages 61-80. Discuss.			**Day 1** *What Is Nature?* (1) Open Bibles and read Job 12:7-8. (2) Read or tell information. Do pages 18-23 or what you can cover. Discuss.		**Day 1** *Writing and Spelling Road to Reading and Thinking* (1) Do your daily assignments for *WSRRT*.	
Day 2 "God With Us" (1) Music, Prayer, MV (Mt 1:21; Jn 8:28; Jn 8:50; Phil 2:5-11) (2) Read and discuss *The Desire of Ages* 21:3-22:1.	**Day 2** *What Is Health* (1) Open Bibles and review De 7:15; De 32:46; and Pr 4:20, 22. (2) Do pages 81-86. Discuss. **END**			**Day 2** *What Is Nature?* (1) Open Bibles and read Ps 143:5. (2) Read or tell information. Do pages 24-30 or what you can cover. **END**		**Day 2** *WSRRT* (1) Do your daily assignments for *WSRRT*. Continue the *WSRRT* but add the Language lessons in whenever it is time to do them. **This will not be repeated.**	

Bible	Health	Math	Music	Nature	H/G/P	Language	Voice
Day 3 "God With Us" (1) Music, Prayer, MV (Mt 1:21; Jn 8:28; Jn 8:50; Phil 2:5-11) (2) Read and discuss *The Desire of Ages* 21:3-22:3.					**Day 3** *What Is H/G/P?* (1) Open Bibles and read He 1:10. (2) Read or tell information. Do pages 1-6 or what you can cover. Discuss. Choose a good mission book to begin reading as a family.	**Day 3** *What Is Language?* (1) Open Bibles and read Col 3:16. (2) Read or tell information. Do pages 1-10 or what you can cover + *WSRRT*. Discuss.	
Day 4 "God With Us" (1) Music, Prayer, MV (Mt 1:21; Jn 8:28; Jn 8:50; Phil 2:5-11) (2) Read and discuss *The Desire of Ages* 22:4-24:1.					**Day 4** *What Is H/G/P?* (1) Open Bibles and read Ps 119:105 & He 13:1. (2) Read or tell information. Do pages 7-14. Discuss.	**Day 4** *What Is Language?* (1) Open Bibles and read Pr 25:11. (2) Read or tell information. Do pages 11-17 + *WSRRT*. Discuss.	**Day 4** *What Is Voice?* (1) Open Bibles and read Ps 105:2. (2) Read or tell information. Do pages 1-4 Discuss.
Day 5 "God With Us" (1) Review. (2) Read and discuss *The Desire of Ages* 24:2-26:3.	**Day 5** *What Is Health?* (1) Review	**Day 5** *What Is Math...?* (1) Review.	**Day 5** *What Is Music?* (1) Review.	**Day 5** *What Is Nature?* (1) Review.	**Day 5** *What Is H/G/P?* (1) Review pages 1-14.	**Day 5** *What Is Language?* (1) Review pages 1-17.	**Day 5** *What Is Voice?* (1) Review pages 1-4.
Week 1 (5) [Month 2] **Lesson 1** **Day 1** "God With Us" (1) Music, Prayer, MV. (2) Read and discuss *The Desire of Ages* 24:2-26:3.					**Day 1** *What Is H/G/P?* (1) Open Bibles and read Jer 10:12. (2) Read or tell information. Do pages 15-25Aa or what you can cover. Discuss.	Do your daily assignments for *WSRRT*. **Day 1** *What Is Language?* (1) Open Bibles and read Jn 1:1. (2) Read or tell information. Do pages 18-22 or what you can cover. Discuss. **END**	**Day 1** *What Is Voice?* (1) Open Bibles and read Ps 32:2. (2) Read or tell information. Do pages 5-8. Discuss. **END**

> If there is any information that the student should know and does not—REVIEW.

Bible	Health	Math	Music	Nature	H/G/P	Language	Voice
Day 2 "God With Us" (1) Music, Prayer, MV. (2) Expand or review any part of the lesson. (Could use section about William Miller in H/G/P.)					**Day 2** *What Is H/G/P?* (1) Open Bibles and read II Pe 1:21. (2) Read or tell information. Do pages 26-47 or what you can cover. Discuss. (Story about "William Miller" may take longer.)	**Day 2** *Writing and Spelling Road to Reading and Thinking* (1) Do your daily assignments for *WSRRT*.	**Day 2** *What Is Voice?* (1) Review
Day 3 "God With Us" (1) Music, Prayer, MV. (2) Expand or review any part of the lesson. (Could use the section in H/G/P, "The Schools of the Prophets.")					**Day 3** *What Is H/G/P?* (1) Open Bibles and read Ja 3:17 & Pr 9:10. (2) Read or tell information. Do pages 48-65 or what you can cover. Discuss.	**Day 3** *Writing and Spelling Road to Reading and Thinking* (1) Do your daily assignments for *WSRRT*.	
Day 4 "God With Us" (1) Music, Prayer, MV. (2) Expand or review any part of the lesson. (Could explain why the Apocrypha books are not included in Bible.) **END**					**Day 4** *What Is H/G/P?* (1) Open Bibles and read Ex 17:14 & Ge 5:22. (2) Read or tell information. Do pages 66-78 or what you can cover. Discuss. **END**	**Day 4** *Writing and Spelling Road to Reading and Thinking* (1) Do your daily assignments for *WSRRT*.	**Day 4-5** Use this time to review anything from lesson 1.

On day 5 review any subject in Lesson 1 that needs a better understanding.

Week 2 | **Month 2**
Lesson 2
Day 1
"The Chosen People"
(1) Music, Prayer, MV.
(2) Read and discuss.

Continue the process with Lesson 2. See the *Road Map and Route Catalogue.*

Music Information

1. Music is broken into two parts:

    A. Music (theory)

    B. Voice (the proper training of correct posture, breathing, and speaking and singing)

2. The voice lesson is especially developed for **Place II - III**. **Place I** can sit in with older brother or sister if they are interested.

3. Scripture music and song books are available through SonLight. Some sheet music is also available.

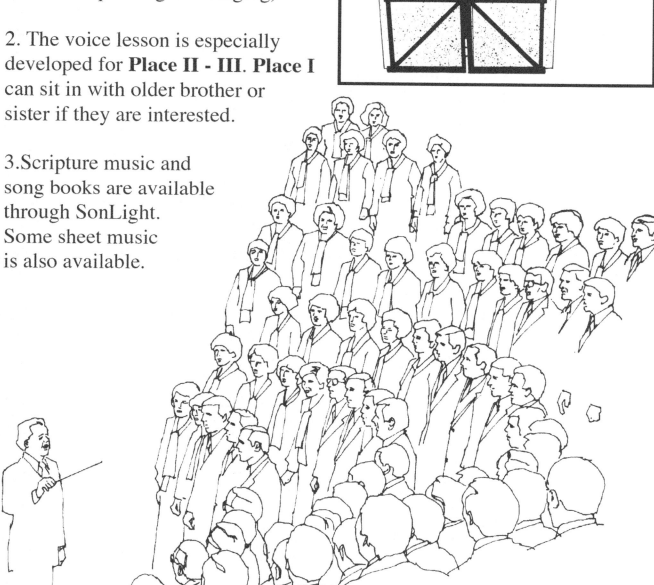

Table of Contents

> "It is a good thing to give thanks
> unto the Lord, and to sing praises
> unto thy name, O most High:
> To shew forth thy <u>lovingkindness</u>...
> Upon an instrument of ten strings,
> and upon the psaltery; upon the harp
> with a solemn sound."
> Psalm 92:1-3

Teacher
Section

Step 1

Study the Bible Lesson and begin to memorize the Memory Verses. Familiarize Yourself With the Character Quality. The student can answer the Bible Review Questions. See page 6. Use the Steps in Bible Study.

Bible Lesson

"God With Us" – Genesis 3:14-15; 12:1-3; Galatians 3:16; Genesis 49:10; Deuteronomy 18:17-19; II Samuel 7:12-17; Ezekiel 21:25-27; Luke 1:32; Isaiah 9:6-7; Psalm 45:1-8; 72:1-11; Isaiah 53; Zechariah 12:10; John 14:9; John 1:1-4; Matthew 1:23

Memory Verses

Matthew 1:23; Matthew 1:20-21; John 8:28; 6:57; 7:18; 8:50; Philippians 2:5-11

Character Quality

Love – an affection of the mind excited by beauty and worth of any kind, or by the qualities of an object; charity.

Antonyms – hate; detestableness; abomination; loathing; scorn; disdainfulness; selfishness

Character Quality Verse

I Corinthians 13:4-7 – *"Charity suffereth long, and is kind; charity envieth not; charity vaunteth not itself, is not puffed up,*

"Doth not behave itself unseemly, seeketh not her own, is not easily provoked, thinketh no evil;

"Rejoiceth not in iniquity, but rejoiceth in the truth;

"Beareth all things, believeth all things, hopeth all things, endureth all things."

Step 2

Understand How To/ And

A. Do the Spelling Cards so the student can begin to build his own spiritual dictionary.

B. Mark the Bible.

C. Evaluate Your Student's Character in relation to the character quality of **love**.

D. Familiarize Yourself with *What is Music?* Notice the Projects.

E. Review the Scripture References for "Music."

F. Notice the Answer Key.

A. Spelling Cards*
Spelling Lists

Music Words
Place I - II - III

bass	enmity
harmony	forever
miscellaneous	head
orchestra	heel
percussion	Judah
principles	kingdom
restore	lawgiver
restorer	**love**
string	peace
symphony	Prophet
woodwind	scepter
	seed
Bible Words	Shiloh
blessing	throne
bruise	woman
Emmanuel	

*See the booklet Spelling from the Scriptures for instructions.

B. How to Mark the Bible

1. Copy the list of Bible texts in the back of the Bible on an empty page as a guide.

2. Go to the first text in the Bible and copy the reference for the next text beside it. Go to the next one and repeat the process until they are all chain referenced.

3. Have the student present the study to family and/or friends.

4. In each student lesson there are one or more sections that have a Bible marking study on the subject studied. (See the student's section, page 51.)

C. Evaluate Your Student's Character

This section is for the purpose of helping the teacher know how to encourage the students in becoming more **loving**. See page 7.

> **Place I = Grades 2-3-4**
> **Place II = Grades 4-5-6**
> **Place III = Grades 6-7-8**

D. Familiarize Yourself with Music — Notice the Projects

Projects

1. As a family, choose a hymn or Scripture song about heaven's music (either one of its principles or music that is in heaven). Sing it every day for worship this week.

2. Choose a favorite Scripture that tells of heavenly music and ask God to give you a tune for it. Remember to follow the 7 principles of heavenly music. Use the sheet on making a Scripture song enclosed with this lesson on page 8. Sing this new Scripture song as a family for your friends and send a copy to SonLight.

3. Gather pictures of different orchestras and their instruments. Put them in a notebook and add Bible texts about orchestras or musicians of the Bible.

4. As a family discuss and make a list of what each person knows concerning heavenly music from the Bible.

5. Interview a Christian musician about what he knows heavenly music to be.

6. If you are not taking private music lessons, check to see what the cost would be, how much you would have to practice, and if your family could afford it.

7. Visit a store that sells pianos or look at the want advertisements to see if there are any for sale. Compare the price of a new piano to that of a used piano. What are the brand names? Do more research to discover what would be excellent brands of pianos. Do you have a piano in your home? What is the brand name?

Notes

E. Review the Scriptures for "Music"

Teacher, read through this section before working on the lesson with the student.

See page 51 in the Student Section.

F. Notice the Answer Key

The answer key for the student book is found on pages 9-10.

Notes

Step 3

Read the Lesson Aim.

Lesson Aim

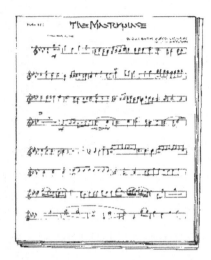

The aim of this lesson is to teach the student that there is music in heaven and that our music needs to be in harmony with heaven's music. In order for our music to be right we must learn the principles of heaven concerning music.

A symphony orchestra has many different instruments. With such a varied combination of tones the music can be very lovely. Yet, the musicians must follow heavenly principles for this to happen.

Music is a wonderful gift from God, but only when the principles of heavenly music are followed.

Step 4

Prepare to begin the Music Lesson.

To Begin the Music Lesson

Plan to go to a store and when you hear the bad music being played, ask the student if this "music" is similar to that which comes forth from holy angels or is sung in heaven. Discuss with the student.

Step 5

Begin the Music lesson. Cover only what can be understood by your student. Make the lessons a family project by involving all in part or all of the lesson. These lessons are designed for the whole family.

Steps in Bible Study

1. Prayer

2. Read the verses/meditate/memorize.

3. Look up key words in *Strong's Concordance* and find their meaning in the Hebrew or Greek diction- ary in the back of that book.

4. Cross reference (marginal reference) with other Bible texts. An excellent study tool is *The Treasury of Scripture Knowledge.*

5. Use Bible custom books for more information on the times.

6. Write a summary of what you have learned from those verses.

7. Mark key thoughts in the margin of your Bible.

8. Share your study with others to reinforce the lessons you have learned.

Bible Review Questions

1. What were the circumstances under which the first promise of a Redeemer was given? (Genesis 3:14-15)

2. What promise was made to Abraham, and what did it mean? (Genesis 12:1-3; Galatians 3:16)

3. Through what tribe of Israel was the Messiah to come? (Genesis 49:10)

4. What promise was given through Moses? (Deuteronomy 18:17-19)

5. Through whom was the permanence of David's kingdom assured? (II Samuel 7:12-17; Ezekiel 21:25-27; Luke 1:32)

6. What exalted ideas concerning the Messiah were made prominent? (Isaiah 9:6, 7; Psalm 45:1-8; 72:1-11)

7. What also was foretold of His relation to sin? (Isaiah 53; Zechariah 12:10)

8. What is the significance of the name which John applies to Christ? (John 1:29; Matthew 1:23)

9. What important facts are stated of Him in John 1:1-4?

    a.

    b.

    c.

10. As part of the great scheme of human redemption, what did the Word become? What is the meaning of the words "became flesh?" (Matthew 1:14)

Notes

Evaluating Your Child's Character

Check the appropriate box for your student's level of development,
or your own, as the case may be.

Maturing Nicely (MN), Needs Improvement (NI), Poorly Developed (PD), Absent (A)

Love

1. "*Charity suffereth long and is kind*" (I Corinthians 13:4). Does my child show a maturity of love that enables him to be kind while suffering from hunger, tiredness, or discomfort?

MN NI PD A
❏   ❏   ❏   ❏

2. When the child encounters people with character deficiencies, is the child's reaction one of **loving** pity and concern instead of condemnation?

MN NI PD A
❏   ❏   ❏   ❏

3. Does your child seem to **love** God more as a result of studying the material contained in the Bible?

MN NI PD A
❏   ❏   ❏   ❏

4. "*Charity...vaunteth not itself; is not puffed up*" (I Corinthians 13:4). Does the child refrain from comparing himself with others? Does he make comments like "I can read better than _____."

MN NI PD A
❏   ❏   ❏   ❏

5. "*Charity...seeketh not her own*" (I Corinthians 13:5). Is the child willing for others to have the best or the most of desirable things?

MN NI PD A
❏   ❏   ❏   ❏

6. "*Love your enemies*" (Matthew 5:44). Does the child initiate reconciliation with or do kind things for those who have hard feelings toward him or who have treated him unfairly?

MN NI PD A
❏   ❏   ❏   ❏

7. "*Charity shall cover the multitude of sins*" (I Peter 4:8). Is the child eager to tell you about the failures of others or does he **lovingly** shield others from exposure where possible to do so with integrity?

MN NI PD A
❏   ❏   ❏   ❏

8. "*Charity...thinketh no evil*" (I Corinthians 13:5). Is the child unsuspecting, ever placing the most favorable construction upon the motives and acts of others?

MN NI PD A
❏   ❏   ❏   ❏

Instructions About How to Compose a Scripture Song

1. Pray for wisdom and inspiration.

2. Choose a Scripture (short at first), including Scripture reference.

3. Talk about any words that need explanation and do a word study from *Strong's Concordance*.

4. Read the Scripture.

5. Clap out each phrase or partial phrase. For example:
I will sing
un-to the Lord
as long as I live
I will sing praise to my God
while I have my be-ing
Psalm One hun-dred four:
Thir-ty-three

"I will sing" has 3 syllables and using the principle of simplicity, it will have one note for each syllable. Clap this several times without saying the words (saying the words will automatically give you the rhythm and this is how you clap it, thinking the words).

If you have a piano or know someone who does, pick out a melody on the black keys (only use the black keys, this will help you avoid the wrong kind of music.)

6. Repeat the above procedure with each phrase.

7. Record the tune on a tape or write out on music paper.

8. Have everyone sing a part.

9. Pray and thank God for the beautiful music. Then use your new song as a prayer response.

It would probably be best to use 4/4 time if you are new at writing music. 4/4 time means that there are four counts to a measure. Try to keep one note per syllable unless you have had more experience.

Answer Key

Page 5

Across:

3 - obedient   12 - humbled
7 - tongue   16 - likeness
10 - servant   17 - name
11 - Lord   20 - Christ

Down:

1 - confess   9 - knee
2 - mind   13 - let
4 - exalted   14 - Jesus
5 - reputation   15 - heaven
6 - God   18 - earth
8 - Glory   19 - death

Page 6

1. Student answer.

2. Yes.
   John 17:16.

3. So that through His sacrifice of love we might be saved.

4. The principles of true music.

5. By learning the 7 principles of heavenly music.

Page 16

1. Through words and music.

2. Yes.
   On earth.

3. To praise the Lord.

Page 17

4. Foolish, Irreverence, out, place.

5. No. Because God is orderly.

6. Student answer.

7. No. Because these are heaven's principles.

8. Disrespectful; inconsiderate; inappreciation; dishonor.

9. No.
   To use musical talent to foster pride and make us the center of attention.

10. Pure, noble, elevated.

11. The melody of praise.

12. By bringing forth glorious sounds as they skillfully sweep their hands over the strings of their harps.

13. To join the heavenly choir when we enter the city of God.

14. Because order is built upon law. Without law you would not know what order was.

15. Perfect order.
    Every area.
    Yes.

16. To follow (obey) all the musical laws.

17. Prayer, Bible study, obeying God.

Page 23

And, the four beasts and four, twenty, before, Lamb, harps, sung, new song, Thou, worthy, Revelation.

Page 24

1. Agreeable sound;
2. Succession of musical notes;
3. Tuneful;
4. Pleasing arrangment of sounds.

Page 28

1. No. Because it hurts our bodies.

2. Sweet and calm.
   Yes.

3. Full and rich.

4. *"Sing unto him a new song; play skilfully with a loud noise."*

5. Pleasant, clear, flowing, silver-toned.

Page 29

6. The repentance of one sinner.

7. Now.

8. Student answer.

Page 29 continued

9. It wearies and shocks your nerves. And also damages our ear drums.

10. No. God always finishes His work, and so must we.

11. Order, obedience, peace, harmony.

12. The unity or oneness of two or more different tones sounding at the same time.

13. Music that is full and rich just means that every note is sounded out with melody and assurance!

14. The music would go on and on.
    Student answer.

15. Before the fall of Lucifer.

16. Christ.
    John 17:21.

Page 30

Word Find Answers:

```
S U O I N O M R A H T E
R E D R O T C E F R E P
H R M M F U L L E S E R
S I L O R D E P R A I A
R A S U O I D O L E M I
C H C I R S W T E E W S
W O R S H I P I L U F E
```

Page 46

See page 31 in the student section for answers.

Gardening Sheet

Lesson ___One___   ___Music___

Title ___"What Is Music?"___

In Season

    Plan your gardens to attract the most birds. Many berry bushes and flowers will bring certain birds. Trees will also provide shelter for the birds. Birds make beautiful music and their flying about add to your garden atmosphere. Their busy flying brings to mind the angels who give **love** and untiring watch-care "to souls that are fallen and unholy."

Out of Season

    Research about how birds can be encouraged to visit your gardens. The birds will teach us many lessons about work in the garden. One such lesson is: "Yet how cheerily they [birds] go about their work! how full of joy are their little songs!" (*Education* 118)

Student Section

Music is the science of harmonious sounds.

What Is Music?

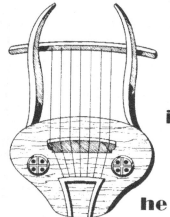

Research
Introduction

**"The LORD thy God
in the midst of thee is mighty;
he will save, he will rejoice
over thee with joy;
he will rest in his love,
he will joy over thee with singing."
Zephaniah 3:17**

In heaven there is music. How do we know? We know this because the Bible speaks of heaven's music a number of times. One of those instances is at the creation of this world. It is written, *"...the morning stars sang together, and all the sons of God shouted for joy"* (Job 38:7). In Revelation we are told of *"harpers harping with their harps"* and the redeemed 144,000 singing unto the Lamb. (See Revelation 14:2-3.) Even God sings, *"The LORD thy God ...will joy over thee with singing"* (Zephaniah 3:17). Indeed there is music in heaven!

**"Sing unto the
LORD with the harp...
and the voice
of a psalm.
With trumpets
and sound of cornets
make a joyful noise
before the LORD,
the King."**

Psalm 98:5-6

Since there is music in God's heavenly family and there is music in God's earthly family, should not the two be in harmony? "The family on earth should be a type of the family in heaven."* Every home "should be a little heaven upon earth...."** God's earthly children should only play or listen to music that is based upon the same principles as heavenly music. Jesus said in John 17:16, *"They [His disciples] are not of the world, even as I am not of the world."* The Christian's music will be different from the world's music.

Jesus came to this earth as an example of the heavenly family. He willingly left the beauty and glory, the adoration and worship of holy beings—which sang praises to His name—to come to this dark, gloomy world. Why? So that through His sacrifice of **love** we might be saved. *"...Jesus...being in the form of God, thought it not robbery to be equal with God: But made himself of no reputation, and took upon him the form of a servant, and was made in the likeness of men: And being found in fashion as a man, he humbled himself, and became obedient unto death, even the death of the cross"* (Philippians 2:5-8).

We see infinite love recorded in the written Word of God. Christ came to interpret the Word by playing it out in a live symphony of loving deeds.

Through His sacrifice of **love** Jesus has linked earth with heaven. "Jesus is the great restorer. In consequence of sin, earth was separated from heaven; but Jesus bridged the impassable gulf, united the fallen world with heaven, linked finite man with the infinite God...."*** One area Christ longs to restore in man are the principles of true music.

In this lesson we are going to learn 7 principles of heavenly music. This will help us know how we can have that music which is in harmony with heaven in our homes. Those 7 principles are:

1. **Form of Worship**
2. **Praise to God**
3. **Perfect Order**
4. **Sweet and Calm**
5. **Full and Rich**
6. **Melodious**

*10 Manuscript Releases 206   **The Adventist Home 15   ***Review and Herald 2/10/1891

The Harps of Heaven

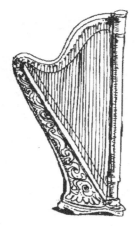

Oh music, angelic and saintly,
    That swells in yon uppermost sphere.
Ye come to earth's dwellers but faintly,
    And we feel the strains, rather than hear.
But the songs that are sung up in glory,
    Will lighten the gloom of the years.
For their echoes breathe out the glad story
    Of a land all unsaddened by tears.

The music of harps 'neath deft fingers,
    Thrilling soft with their promise of peace,
In the hearts of world-weary lingers,
    'Foretelling the soul's glad release.
Foretelling the wondrous forever,
    That shall thrill with the rapture of heaven,
Of the glorified life that shall never
    To burdens of sorrow be given.

Where smiles light the beautiful faces
    Of the dear ones who'll gather above.
Where the storms of the earth leave no traces
    On the brows all transfigured by love.
    —*Unknown*

Reinforce
Love
Place I - II - III

L Philippians 2:5-11

I Isaiah 53
John 8:50

"**The contemplation of the <u>love</u> of God manifested in His Son will stir the heart and arouse the powers of the soul as nothing else can.**"

The Desire of Ages 478

V  John 3:16

"**It was He [Christ]... that filled the earth with beauty, and the air with song. And upon all things in earth, and air, and sky, He wrote the message of the Father's <u>love</u>.**"

The Desire of Ages 20

E Psalm 40:8
John 1:14

Color these letters.
Look up these texts that explain <u>love</u> and read them.

O Great is Thy Love!

Look up Philippians 2:5-11 and do the crossword puzzle below.

ACROSS

3. Jesus became this unto death.
7. Every one of these shall confess that Jesus is Lord.
10. Jesus took upon Him the form of a _____.
11. Jesus Christ is L__ __ __.
12. Jesus _____ Himself.
16. Jesus was made in the _____ of men.
17. Jesus was given one of these which is above every other.
20. Jesus is the C__ __ __ __ __.

DOWN

1. Every tongue shall do this.
2. We are to let this be in us.
4. God highly _____ Jesus.
5. Jesus made Himself of no-_____.
6. Jesus Christ was in the form of G_____.
8. ...to the _____ of God the Father.
9. Every _____ shall bow.
13. _____this mind be in you.
14. _____ Christ is Lord.
15. ...every knee should bow, of things in _____.
18. ...every knee should bow, ...and things in _____.
19. Jesus became obedient unto _____.

Review
Place I - II - III

1. What are two Bible texts that tell us there is music in heaven? Write them out.

I._____

_____

_____

II._____

_____

_____

2. Is the music of Christians to be based on the principles of heavenly music? Where does the Bible tell us this?

3. Why was Jesus willing to leave the glory of heaven?

4. What was one area Christ longed to restore in man?

5. How can we know if the music we are listening to or playing is in harmony with heaven?

"And the ransomed of the Lord shall return,
and come to Zion with songs
and everlasting joy upon their heads:
they shall obtain joy and gladness,
and sorrow and sighing shall flee away."

Isaiah 35:10

Research
1. Form of Worship

"...I heard the voice of harpers harping with their harps: And they sung as it were a new song before the throne...."
Revelation 14:2-3

In the courts above God is not worshiped with words only. Instruments of praise are also used to express **love** to God. *"And I beheld, and I heard the voice of many angels round about the throne... Saying with a loud voice, Worthy is the Lamb that was slain to receive power, and riches, and wisdom, and strength, and honour, and glory, and blessing"* (Revelation 5:11-12). *"...I heard the voice of harpers harping with their harps: And they sung as it were a new song <u>before the throne</u>..."* (Revelation 14:2-3). "...All the angels <u>worship</u> Him, and they bow in adoration before Him, and they touch their golden harps, and raise their voices in praise...."*

When the redeemed throng shall at last stand in the holy city, one of the gifts God presents to each one is a beautiful harp. These ransomed souls will bring forth glorious sounds as they skillfully sweep their hands over the strings of the harp <u>in worship to God</u>. Those beautiful sounds will be heard again and again throughout eternity. Truly, *"...Eye hath not seen, <u>nor ear heard</u>, neither have entered into the heart of man, the things which God hath prepared for them that **love** him"* (I Corinthians 2:9).

Where will the redeemed learn to play in one accord with heaven? It will be here on this earth. The Lord declares, "I will meet with thee, and I will commune with thee" (Exodus 25:22). It is here that God begins communing with us and teaching us about heavenly things. "Heaven's communion

*The Ellen G. White 1888 Materials 127

Reflect

"In order to be at home in heaven, we must have heaven enshrined in our hearts here."

God's Amazing Grace 251

begins on earth. We learn here its keynote."* All who will may receive one of these heavenly harps. By the sacrifice of **love** Jesus made upon the cross, these golden harps have been promised to everyone who will be faithful and true to God. *"In this was manifested the **love** of God toward us, because that God sent his only begotten Son into the world, that we might live through him"* (I John 4:9). "He gave His life for you. He bore the penalty of sin and transgression for every son and daughter of Adam that they should not perish if they believe in Him, but have everlasting life."**

The music that we play here on earth should be a <u>form of worship</u> to God, as the music played in heaven. In other words, we should not play or sing foolish tunes. Irreverence when playing upon an instrument or singing is out of place. The Bible says, *"It is a good thing to give thanks unto the LORD...Upon an instrument of ten*

strings, and upon the psaltery; upon the harp with a <u>solemn sound</u>" (Psalm 92:1, 3). "No one who has an indwelling Saviour will dishonor Him before others by producing strains from a musical instrument which call the mind from God and Heaven to light and trifling things. Music was made to serve a holy purpose, to lift the thoughts to that which is pure, noble, and elevating, and to awaken in the soul devotion and gratitude to God."***

When you play music or sing a song, are your thoughts uplifted to pure, noble, and elevating themes? Do you have an attitude of <u>worship</u> or one of foolishness? Is the music itself a <u>form of worship</u> to God?

> **"All the earth shall <u>worship</u> thee, and shall sing unto thee; they shall sing to thy name."**
>
> **Psalm 66:4**

> **"I will...sing praise unto thee. I will <u>worship</u> toward thy holy temple, and praise thy name for thy lovingkindness and for thy truth: for thou hast magnified thy word above all thy name...Yea, they shall sing in the ways of the LORD: for great is the glory of the LORD."**
> **Psalm 138:1-2, 5**

*Youth Instructor 3/29/1904   **8 Manuscript Releases 210   ***Sons and Daughters of God 179

What Is Music? – Student – Page 8

The Harp In Heaven

One of the sweetest recollections of my girlhood is a beautiful reply my mother once made to me, when my heart was swelling with childish grief.

I had just returned from the house of a wealthy neighbor, who had kindly given me the use of their piano for a few hours every day, to gratify my extreme love for music. Our own cottage home looked so plain in contrast with the one I had just left, and no piano within its walls. I laid my head upon the table and gave vent to my overflowing heart. I felt grieved, and perhaps a little angry, that we were unable to afford the one thing I desired above all others—a piano—and expressed my feelings to my mother.

Never shall I forget her sweet, gentle, tone, as she simply replied, "Never mind, if you cannot have a piano on earth, you may have a harp in heaven." Instantly the whole current of feelings was changed. Earthly things dwindled into insignificance, and the harp in heaven, with its golden strings, became the object of my desire. I felt reproved for my re-pinings against Providence that had placed me in a humble home, and from that moment the enjoyments of Heaven seemed far to outweigh all the pleasures of earth.

That beautiful reply has followed me all my life, or rather has gone before me like a bright guiding star, lifting my thoughts above this transient life, and summoning to my spirit's vision the bright-scenes in that land of life and light. Oh! that harp in heaven, how my soul longs for one breath of its rich melody.

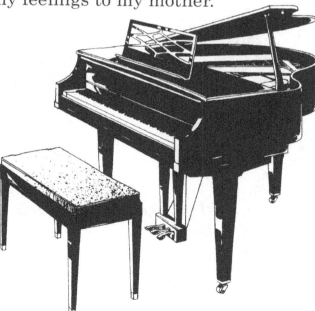

2. Praise To God

"And suddenly there was with the angel a multitude of the heavenly host praising God, and saying, Glory to God in the highest, and on earth peace, good will toward men."

Luke 2:13-14

"The melody of praise is the atmosphere of heaven; and when heaven comes in touch with the earth, there is music and song— 'thanksgiving, and the voice of melody.'" * One of the times this happened was when Jesus came down from heaven to this earth and became "God with us." "The whole plain was lighted up with the bright shining of the hosts of God. Earth was hushed, and heaven stooped to listen to the song,—

'Glory to God in the highest,
And on earth peace, good will
toward men.'" **

Nothing in heaven dishonors God—including the music. Everything there only exalts, honors, and praises Him. We must tune our hearts to this kind of music if heaven is to be our final home. The heart that is not given to God does not naturally praise Him. Our natural tendency is to use musical talent to foster pride and make us the center of attention. Many there are who employ the gift of music to

"Sing unto the Lord, O ye saints of his, and give thanks at the remembrance of his holiness."

Psalm 30:4

exalt self instead of using it to glorify God. This type of music produces an unmusical sound in heaven's ears. The laws of heavenly music are not being followed, so the sound cannot be musical.

King David made instruments with a special purpose in mind. Do you know what it was? It was to praise the Lord. "...*The Levites also with instruments of music of the LORD, which David the king had made to praise the LORD...*" (II Chronicles 7:6). The Bible tells us to "*Praise the*

*The Youth Instructor 3/29/1904   **The Desire of Ages 48*

LORD *with harp: sing unto him with the psaltery and an instrument of ten strings"* (Psalm 33:2). How are you using the gift of music?

When sin is forever ended and the redeemed stand within the holy city, songs of triumph will be heard in praise to God. *"And I saw as it were a sea of glass mingled with fire: and them that had gotten the victory over the beast...stand on the sea of glass, having the harps of God. And they sing the song of Moses the servant of God, and the song of the Lamb, saying, Great and marvellous are thy works, Lord God Almighty; just and true are thy ways, thou King of saints. Who shall not fear thee, O Lord, and glorify thy name? for thou only art holy: for all nations shall come and worship before thee; for thy judgments are made manifest"* (Revelation 15:2-4). Heaven will seem to overflow with joy and praise! **"Love** has conquered. The lost is found."* "The work of redemption will be complete. In the place where sin abounded, God's grace much more abounds."**

With the scene before us of the matchless **love** of God and what heaven gave for our salvation, how can we not use music only for His praise and honor? How can we selfishly refuse to bestow it upon Him who has done so much for us?

"Whoso offereth praise glorifieth me..." (Psalm 50:23). "Let your conversation, your music, your songs all praise Him who has done so much for us. Praise God here, and then you will be fitted to join the heavenly choir when you enter the city of God."***

Remind

When you are asked by father to wash his truck and you do not want to do it, let not your words utter one complaint. But make your work pleasant by singing "Praise to the Lord," or another song of praise.

"I will also praise thee with the psaltery, even thy truth, O my God: unto thee will I sing with the harp, O thou Holy One of Israel."

Psalm 71:22

The Desire of Ages 835   **The Desire of Ages* 26   ****My Life Today* 91

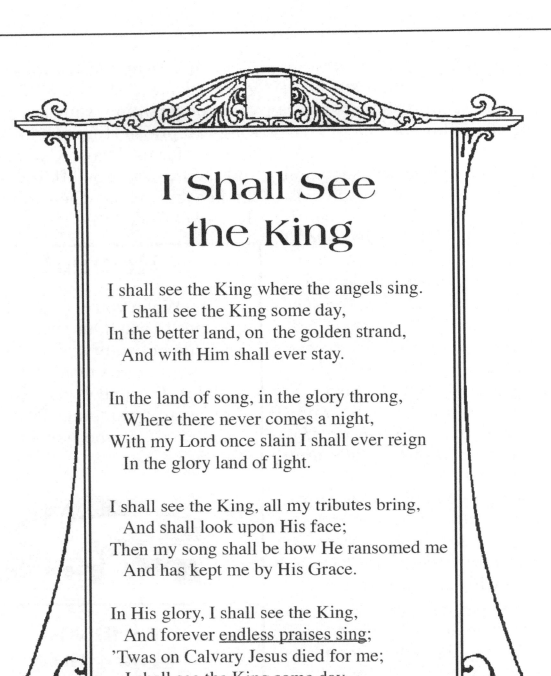

I Shall See
the King

I shall see the King where the angels sing.
   I shall see the King some day,
In the better land, on the golden strand,
   And with Him shall ever stay.

In the land of song, in the glory throng,
   Where there never comes a night,
With my Lord once slain I shall ever reign
   In the glory land of light.

I shall see the King, all my tributes bring,
   And shall look upon His face;
Then my song shall be how He ransomed me
   And has kept me by His Grace.

In His glory, I shall see the King,
   And forever <u>endless praises sing</u>;
'Twas on Calvary Jesus died for me;
   I shall see the King some day.

—Unknown

"Even so, come, Lord Jesus."
Revelation 22:20

3. Perfect Order
"Let all things be done decently and in order."
"For God is not the author of confusion...."
I Corinthians 14:40, 33

There is no such thing as chaos (complete disorder) in heaven, *"For God is not the author of confusion..."* (I Corinthians 14:33). "God is a God of <u>order</u>."* We can see this in the history of Israel. As the Israelites journeyed in the wilderness, their encampment was always arranged in <u>perfect order</u>. Each tribe had a specified position. The Lord had commanded: *"Every man of the children of Israel shall pitch by his own standard, with the ensign of their father's house: far off about the tabernacle of the congregation shall they pitch." "As they*

encamp, so shall they set forward, every man <u>in his place</u> by their standards" (Numbers 2:2, 17). "God gave the Israelites special directions concerning the arrangement of their camp, that all might be in <u>perfect order</u>. And everything connected with the tabernacle was designed to impress the people with the majesty and holiness of God, and the purity He requires of all who engage in His service."** For Israel to enjoy the presence of a holy God it was necessary that <u>perfect order</u> and purity be maintained. *"The Lord thy God walketh in the midst of thy*

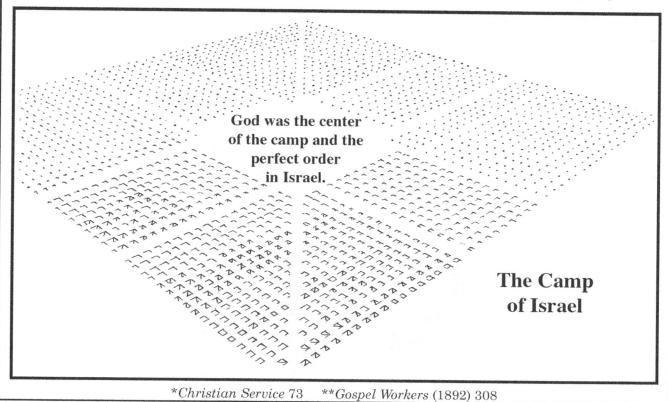

God was the center of the camp and the perfect order in Israel.

The Camp of Israel

*Christian Service 73   **Gospel Workers (1892) 308

camp, to deliver thee, and to give up thine enemies before thee; therefore shall thy camp be holy" (Deuteronomy 23:14). If you desire God to walk in your home and church, then you also must have your home and church in <u>perfect order.</u>

    <u>Order</u> is built upon law. When you clean your closet and put your shoes in <u>order</u> by neatly lining them up, you are following law. That law tells you that your shoes are not in <u>order</u> when they are thrown in a pile in your closet.

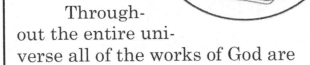

    Throughout the entire universe all of the works of God are

manifest in system and <u>order</u>. "<u>Order</u> is the law of heaven, and it should be the law of God's people on the earth."* "Everything connected with heaven is in <u>perfect order</u>."** You can be connected (united) with heaven by prayer, Bible study, and obeying God. When this connection is formed, <u>perfect order</u> will be clearly seen in the life. And the music that ascends to God from His children will be of that character also—<u>orderly</u>.

Reflect

In an orchestra <u>perfect order</u> in the musical performances is essential. Each musician must abide by the laws of music for this to be achieved.

*Testimonies to Ministers 26 **Christian Service 73

What does it mean for music to be in <u>perfect order</u>? When musicians follow certain musical laws or rules that God has set up, the sound that is brought forth is <u>orderly</u>. For example, in later lessons we are going to be learning about key signatures. In music you can play in different keys to produce different sounds. So, for the sake of illustrating, we will say that two musicians—a pianist and a violinist—will play together the hymn, "Lead Us, Heavenly Father." They play the first verse of the hymn in <u>perfect order</u>—following all the musical laws—and the sound is **lovely**. As they begin the second verse the violinist, without warning, decides to play in a different key. What do you suppose would happen? The sound that would come forth would no longer be <u>orderly</u>, and chaotic noise would be heard!

The musical staff is something that holds musical notes and symbols in their place on the paper. Without this staff music could not be <u>orderly</u>. Why? Because you would not know whether to play an A note or a C note. The notes and symbols on the paper would be meaningless. As Jesus walked upon earth He was upheld (as the staff holds notes and symbols) by the Father and His life was therefore in <u>perfect order</u>.

A blessing attends those who listen to music that is played in <u>perfect order</u>. The sound is uplifting and **lovely**. This can remind you of the blessing God gives all who obey His law, the ten commandments. *"A blessing, if ye obey the commandments of the LORD your God..."* (Deuteronomy 11:27). In John 14:15 Jesus said, *"If ye **love** me, keep my commandments."* This includes the laws of music. Jesus came to this

Reinforce

Demonstrate what it means to play in different keys on the piano.
If you do not have a piano ask a friend to show you.

Christ taught man how to glorify God by <u>ordering</u> His life according to the principles of the kingdom of heaven. "<u>Order</u> my steps in thy word." Psalm 119:133

sin-polluted world and "gave us an example of [that kind of **loving**] obedience; as the Son of God, He gave us power to obey."* *"Behold, I give unto you power..."* said our Saviour in Luke 10:19. "Satan represents God's law of **love** as a law of selfishness. He declares that it is impossible for us to obey its precepts...As He [Jesus] went about doing good, and healing all who were afflicted by Satan, He made plain to men the character of God's law and the nature of His service. His life testifies that it is possible for us also to obey the law of God."* God's law brings <u>order</u> to our life.

As you play an instrument or listen to music, be sure that it reflects the laws of heavenly music that are in <u>perfect order</u>. Anytime musicians do not follow law and <u>order</u> in their performance you can be sure that it is not the kind of music God approves of. *"For God is not the author of confusion...* [Therefore] *let <u>all</u> things be done decently and in order"* (I Corinthians 14:33, 40).

Reinforce

To demonstrate disorderly music, take two different music tapes. Play them at the same time. Then play just one at a time. When is it that you hear lovely music, when both tapes are playing at the same time or when only one is playing?

Remind

After breakfast when you wash the dishes and put them away in <u>order</u> (the silverware in its proper drawer, the plates stacked in their place, etc.) be reminded how heavenly music is also to have a <u>perfect order</u>.

Review
Place I - II - III
1-3 Principles
of Heavenly Music

1. In heaven how is God worshiped?

2, Will the ransomed already know how to play in one accord with heaven?

   Where did they learn to do this?

3. What did king David make instruments for?

4. Fill in the blanks:

We should not play or sing

_____ tunes. _____

when playing upon an instru-

ment or singing is _____

of _____.

5. In heaven is there any disorder? Why or why not?

6. Write on the lines below some-thing in the Bible which shows per-fect order (other than the Israelite camp).

_____

_____

_____

_____

7. Does God approve of music that does not abide by these principles that we have just covered? Why?

Place II - III

8. What does irreverence mean? Look it up in a dictionary.

9. Is our natural tendency to praise God with musical talent?

What is our natural tendency?

10. What will happen to your thoughts when you listen to music

that is in harmony with heaven's principles?

They will be uplifted to

_____, _____, and

_____ themes.

11. What is the atmosphere of heav-en?

Place III

12. How will the redeemed worship God?

13. If we praise God here in our con-versation, music, and songs, what will we be fitted for?

14. Why do you need law before you can have order?

15. What will be clearly seen in your life when you are connected with heaven?

In how many areas?

Does this include music?

16. What does it mean for music to be in perfect order?

17. List three ways that you are connected with heaven.

I._____

II._____

III._____

Research
4. Sweet and Calm

"And after the earthquake a fire; but the LORD was not in the fire: and after the fire a <u>still</u> <u>small</u> <u>voice</u>."
I Kings 19:12

On the lines below list three things that are sweet or calm. (For example: the fragrance of a rose is sweet and a running brook is calming.)

1. _____

2. _____

3. _____

Now list three things that are harsh or discordant. (For example: unkind words are harsh.)

1. _____

2. _____

3. _____

Which term would heavenly music fall into, sweet and calm, or harsh and discordant? _____

_____

The music which comes forth from angel harps is <u>calming</u>. It does not grate upon the ear for every tone is filled with <u>sweet</u> strains. In such music holy angels express their **love** to the Creator.

It is written that God speaks with a <u>still</u> (calm) <u>small</u> (sweet-sounding) <u>voice</u>. (See I Kings 19:12.) *"How <u>sweet</u> are thy words unto my taste! yea, <u>sweeter</u> than honey to my mouth!"* (Psalm 119:103). God's voice is also described *"as the sound of many waters"* (Revelation 1:15), which is a <u>calming</u> sound. Why would we want to respond to God's gentle call with word or music that is harsh

Angels we have heard on high,
Singing sweetly through the night,
And the mountains in reply
Echoing their brave delight.

or discordant? It is the perfect, calm, sweet strains of our words and our music that are acceptable and pleasing to God. He tells us, *"Be still* [calm] *and know that I am God"* (Psalm 46:10).

An opposite of sweet is harsh or loud-sounding. Music that is too noisy wearies and shocks your nerves. It also damages your ear drums. Once your ear drums are damaged they never repair themselves. *"I beseech you therefore, brethren, by the mercies of God, that ye present your bodies a living sacrifice, holy, acceptable unto God, which is your reasonable service"* (Romans 12:1). God is not honored when we hurt our bodies by listening to music that is too loud or harsh sounding.

In the heavenly courts, before Jesus came to this earth, He knew that His life on earth would be made hard by those who did not **love** Him. Yet, He still came to this world. Why? Because He looked into the future and saw all who would be saved by His sacrifice, and, oh, how sweet was this thought to Him! *"Looking unto Jesus the author and finisher of our faith; who for the joy that was set before him endured the cross, despising the shame, and is set down at the right hand of the throne of God"* (Hebrews 12:2). "His **love** is without a parallel. It did not stop short of anything...."* "The matchless **love** of God for a world that did not **love** Him!**

Music can damages your ear drums. Once your ear drums are damaged they never repair themselves.

Reflect

Many there are in this world that are drinking from a fountain that sends forth bitter waters. Jesus came to this world to bring within the reach of all the sweet water of life. What love He has for lost humanity!

*5 Bible Commentary 1101 **Steps to Christ 15*

5. Full and Rich

"Sing, O ye heavens; for the Lord hath done it: shout ye lower parts of the earth: break forth into singing, ye mountains, O forest, and every tree therein: for the Lord hath redeemed Jacob, and glorified himself in Israel."
Isaiah 44:23

There is another side to heavenly music that balances the sweet and calm principle. It is being full and rich. A complete symphony orchestra can do a beautiful job of producing music like that!

When music follows this principle it just means that every note is sounded out with melody and assurance! In the holy city angels gather with their harps in hand and make heaven's arches ring with the greatness of full, rich music. There are no incomplete strains because they know that *"he which hath begun a good work in you will perform* [finish] *it until the day of Jesus Christ"* (Philippians 1:6). Completion of sav-

ing people from their sins is why even *"the Lord thy God...will joy over thee with singing"* (Zephaniah 3:17).

Whenever music is played and stops abruptly, leaving you anticipating or waiting for more, it is unfinished. It is incomplete, it is not full. God Himself always finishes what He starts. In the creation of this world the Bible tells us that God completed it, *"Thus the heavens and the earth were finished..."* (Genesis 2:1). When Jesus was upon earth and His ministry was drawing to a close He said, *"I have glorified thee* [the Father] *on the earth: I have finished the work which thou gavest me to do."* (John 17:4). And

upon the cross Jesus cried out, *"It is finished..."* (John 19:30). All who follow Christ will also finish what they start. And they will not play music which does not come to a completion. This is called being resolved. (When resolving a piece of music, the musician will be sure to play that last note, or notes, and thereby leave the listener with a satisfied feeling. This is important, because if a musical piece is missing the last note, or notes, the listener feels as though he is left hanging and unfulfilled.)

"When the conflict is forever ended, what songs of praise will <u>burst forth</u> [<u>full</u> and <u>rich</u>] from the redeemed host! That will indeed be music. Without a discordant note, the <u>rich</u>, <u>full</u> anthem will arise from immortal voices, *'Worthy, worthy is the Lamb.'"** "The work of redemption will be <u>complete</u>. In the place where

sin abounded, God's grace much more abounds...And through the endless ages as the redeemed walk in the light of the Lord, they will praise Him for His unspeakable Gift—

Immanuel, *'God with us.'"***

"Sing, O ye heavens; for the Lord hath done it...the Lord hath redeemed Jacob, and glorified himself in Israel" (Isaiah 44:23).

"Sing unto him a new song; <u>play skilfully with a loud [full and rich] noise</u>."
Psalm 33:3

Reinforce
Sing the hymn, "Come, Let us Sing."

*Signs of the Times 2/14/1900   **The Desire of Ages 26

Come, Let us Sing

Reinforce
Place II - III
Use the key to fill in the blanks.

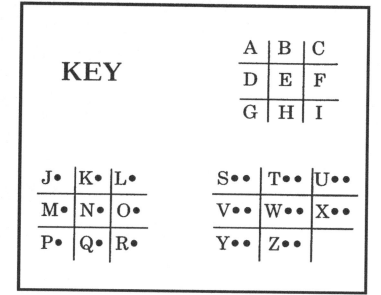

KEY

A	B	C
D	E	F
G	H	I

J•	K•	L•
M•	N•	O•
P•	Q•	R•

S••	T••	U••
V••	W••	X••
Y••	Z••	

"_____ . . . _____ _____ _____ _____ _____

_____ and _____ elders fell down _____ the

_____ _____ _____

_____, having every one of them _____ . . .

_____ _____

And they _____ a _____ _____, saying,

_____ _____ _____

_____ art _____ ..." (_____ 5:8-9).

6. Melodious

"Speaking to yourselves in psalms and hymns and spiritual songs, singing and making melody in your heart to the Lord."
Ephesians 5:19

Melodious, what does that mean? On the lines below write four definitions for melodious. Use a dictionary.

1. _____

2. _____

3. _____

4. _____

There are a handful of words that describe melodious. A few of them are: pleasant, clear, flowing, silver-toned, golden-toned, dulcet, and sweet-sounding. Does that sound beautiful? Imagine what melodious heavenly music sounds like! Can you think of a time in the Bible when melodious music from heaven was heard by the ears of man? Remember when holy angels **lovingly** announced the birth of Jesus to the shepherds!

What would be the opposite of melodious music? It would be noise that was hard, distasteful, unpleasant, sour-sounding, and black-toned. Such noise, which is wrongfully called music by some, is not at all what the shepherd's heard from the angels just come from the presence of God. It has been written concerning this event, "Then was the melody of heaven heard by mortal ears, and the heavenly choir swept back to heaven as they closed their ever memorable anthem."*

Isaiah heard the melodious music of heaven. In a vision he beheld seraphims and listened to the triumphant song of praise that was echoed from one to another in the melodious chant, *"Holy, holy, holy, is the Lord of hosts"* (Isaiah 6:3). What a song that must have been!

Do you like to rest? Resting is important, even in melodious music. "But why would melodious music

> ## "I will sing of thy power; yea, I will sing aloud of thy mercy."
> ### Psalm 59:16

*My Life Today 363

What Is Music? – Student – Page 24

need resting points?" you might wonder. If there were no rests or pauses the music would go on and on, making the listener very weary. Have you ever listened to someone talk who did not stop or pause even once? They just go to one subject after the other and it is hard to keep up with them. After a while you do not want to listen to them talk anymore. This is what it is like when music does not have rests. Let this remind you of how Jesus rested in the **loving** care of His heavenly Father all through His life on earth. Are you resting in Jesus? When we do not rest in Jesus it wearies those around us and ourselves.

The Bible says, *"...there is joy in the presence of the angels of God over one sinner that repenteth"* (Luke 15:10). "The repentance of one soul sends inexpressible joy through all the host of heaven. Melody is called forth from every harp and every voice in glorious anthems because another name is registered in the book of life, another light is kindled to shine amid the moral darkness of this corrupt world."* *"Praise ye the Lord. Praise ye the Lord from the heavens: praise him...all his hosts.... Praise him, ye heavens of heavens..."* (Psalm 148:1-2, 4).

You do not have to wait until you reach heaven to sing melodious
*Our High Calling 89

music with the heavenly host. You can start now as you study, work, and serve others! Read Ephesians 5:19.

I Will Sing of Jesus' Love

I will sing of Jesus' **love**,
Sing of Him who first **loved** me;
For He left bright worlds above,
And died on Calvary.

Ere a tear had dim'd mine eyes,
Jesus' tears for me did flow;
Ere my first faint prayer could rise,
He had prayed in tones of woe.

O the depths of **love** divine!
Earth or heaven can never know
How that sins as dark as mine
Can be made as white as snow.

Nothing good for Him I've done;
How could He such **love** bestow?
Lord, I own my heart is won,
Help me now my **love** to show.

I will sing of Jesus' **love**,
Endless praise my heart shall give;
He has died that I might live—
I will sing His **love** to me.
—F. E. Belden

7. Harmonious

"...The trumpeters and singers were as one [harmony], to make one sound [harmony] to be heard in praising and thanking the Lord...."
II Chronicles 5:13

"In heaven there is perfect order, perfect obedience, perfect peace and harmony."* Harmony in music is the unity or oneness of two or more different tones sounding at the same time, like a symphony orchestra playing in unison.

One of the elements that is critical in order for two or more musicians to harmonize is timing. If even one of the musicians decides not to follow the outlined time signature, musical harmony is impossible. We must be in harmony with Christ as He was with the Father. *"I and my Father are one"* (John 10:30).

"Music forms a part of God's worship in the courts above, and we should endeavor, in our songs of praise, to approach as nearly as possible to the harmony of the heavenly choirs."** Is your music in harmony with unfallen beings, angels, and God's laws for music?

Before the fall of Lucifer (Satan) in heaven, every created being acknowledged the allegiance of **love**, and there was perfect harmony throughout God's entire universe as a result. "While **love** to God was supreme, **love** for one another was

Reflect

Human nature is like a musical instrument responding to the touch of the player. The ignorant hand will bring forth discordant sounds, while a proficient touch creates beautiful chords in perfect harmony.

—Unknown

*Christian Education 237   **Patriarchs and Prophets 594

Reflect

The sweetest music in the world is the music of a life in <u>harmony</u> with the law of God.
—Bert Rhoads

confiding and unselfish. There was no note of discord to mar the celestial <u>harmonies</u>," just like good music. But when Lucifer began little by little "to indulge the desire for self-exaltation...the perfect <u>harmony</u> of heaven was broken."* "Sin originated in self-seeking."** *"Thine [Lucifer's] heart was lifted up because of thy beauty, thou hast corrupted thy wisdom by reason of thy brightness..."* (Ezekiel 28:17).

Selfishness was the motive behind our first parent's fall and sin–disharmony–entered this world. "By disobedience he [Adam] was brought under bondage. Thus a discordant element, born of selfishness, entered man's life. Man's will and God's will no longer <u>harmonized</u>. Adam had united with the disloyal forces, and self-will took the field."*** Therefore the Son of God chose to come to this earth so that He might "reach to the depths of man's degradation and woe, and restore the repenting, believing soul to <u>harmony</u> with God."**** *"In this was manifested the **love** of God toward us, because that God sent his only begotten Son into the world, that we might live through him"* (I John 4:9).

One day soon, <u>one</u> pulse of <u>harmony</u> and gladness will beat through the entire universe, as it did before sin. "From the minutest atom to the greatest world, all things, animate and inanimate, in their unshadowed beauty and perfect joy, [will] declare that God is **love**."*****

"The Lord is anxious to save us. He is anxious that everything separating us from Him should be put away, that our hearts may beat in <u>unison</u> with heaven." Jesus prayed, *"That they all may be <u>one</u>; as thou, Father, art in me, and I in thee, that they also may be <u>one</u> in us..."* (John 17:21). "It is time to be in <u>harmony</u> with God," and this includes our music.******

*Patriarchs and Prophets 35   **Desire of Ages 21   ***Signs of the Times 6/13/1900
****That I May Know Him 18   *****God's Amazing Grace 361   ******1 Sermons and Talks 378

Reflect
One Sin

"If one note in the organ be out of key, or harsh in tone, it mars the whole tune. All the other reeds may be in harmony; but the one defective reed destroys the sweetness of all the rest. In every tune it makes discord somewhere. Its noise jars out into every other note. And so one sin destroys the harmony of a whole life. A boy or girl may be obedient, industrious, and honest; but ill-temper is a jarring reed that touches every grace with chill and discord. Let every affection and every thought and every word and every action, be right; then there is music in the life."

—*Unknown*

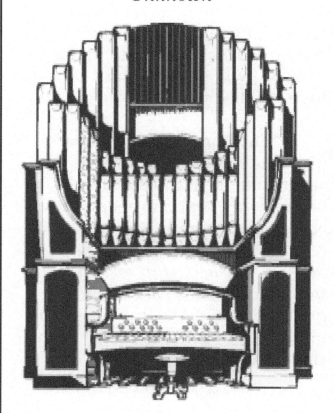

Hand to hand <u>united,</u>
Heart to heart <u>as one,</u>
Let us still keep marching
Till our journey's done,
Till we see the angels
Come in glory down,
With the shining garments
And the victor's crown.

—Mrs. M. A. Kidder

Review
Place I - II - III

4-7 Principles of Heavenly Music

1. Is God honored by very loud music? Why?

2. What is the opposite of loud, discordant, harsh music?

    Is this kind of music heavenly?

3. What balances the sweet and calm principle of heavenly music?

4. On the lines below write the Scripture in Psalm 33:3.

_____

_____

_____

5. What are four of the words that describe melodious?

6. What event especially makes melody in heaven?

7. When is the time for you to be in harmony with God?

8. Is your music in harmony with the 7 principles of heavenly music?

Place II - III

9. When we listen to music that is too loud, what happens?

10. Is unresolved music heavenly? Why?

11. Fill in the blanks:

"In heaven there is perfect

_____, perfect _____,

perfect _____ and _____."

12. What does harmony mean?

Place III

13. Explain to your teacher what is full and rich music.

14. If there were no rests or pauses in music what would happen?

Would this weary you?

15. When was there perfect harmony in the entire universe?

16. In God's word, whom are we told that we need to especially be in harmony with?

Where does the Bible say this?

Reinforce
Place II - III

WORD SEARCH
Find in the box of letters
the words from the word list. Circle them.
Remember all of the principles of heavenly music.

WORD LIST
WORSHIP
PRAISE
PERFECT ORDER
SWEET
CALM
FULL
RICH
MELODIOUS
HARMONIOUS

```
S U O I N O M R A H T E
R E D R O T C E F R E P
H R M M F U L L E S E R
S I L O R D E P R A I A
R A S U O I D O L E M I
C H C I R S W T E E W S
W O R S H I P I L U F E
```

The Symphony Orchestra

Conductor

Strings

Woodwinds

Brass

Percussion

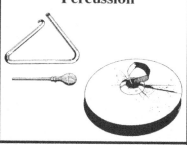

Miscellaneous

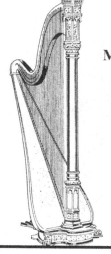

"Make a joyful noise unto the Lord, all ye lands."
Psalm 100:1

Research

♪ ♫ ♪ The Symphony Orchestra

"And David and all of Israel played before the Lord with all their might, and with singing, and with harps, and with psalteries, and with timbrels, and with cymbals, and with trumpets."
I Chronicles 13:8

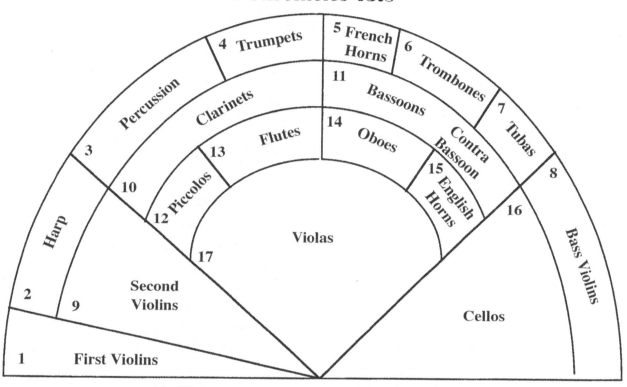

19 Piano   18 Conductor

What is a symphony orchestra? It is a group of musicians who play together on various instruments which enable them to produce a full range of musical sounds. There are string, woodwind, brass, and percussion instruments. The musicians are divided into four main sections or groups – (1) strings, (2) woodwind, (3) brass, and (4) percussion. The instruments are pitched at different ranges just as are the voices in a chorus. Pitched means that some are higher and some are lower in sound. A conductor coordinates all these different sounds together so they will make beautiful music! God gave us Jesus out of **love** to conduct His people that they may make beautiful music in harmony for Him!

King David played in an orchestra. It was not a symphony orchestra, but you could call it an orchestra. Read again I Chronicles 13:8.

An earthly orchestra that plays pure music will follow the 7 principles of heavenly music.

Orchestra Sections

(1) The String Section

"The Lord was ready to save me: therefore we will sing my songs to the stringed instruments all the days of our life in the house of the Lord."
Isaiah 38:20

This is the heart of the symphony orchestra. It contains more than half of the musicians playing— 20 to 32 <u>violins</u>, 8 to 10 violas, 8 to 10 cellos, and 6 to 10 string basses. The violinists are divided into two groups. The first violins play the highest-pitched part in the string section and the second violins play

the next highest part. The leading first violinist is the concertmaster of the orchestra. The concertmaster leads out in tuning the instruments and may also act as the assistant conductor.

(2) The Woodwind Section

"Ye shall have a song, as in the night when a holy solemnity is kept; and gladness of heart, as when one goeth with a pipe to come into the mountain of the Lord...."
Isaiah 30:29

This consists chiefly of flutes, <u>oboes</u>, clarinets, and bassoons. The symphony orchestra has from 2 to 4 of each of these instruments.

(3) The Brass Section

**"With trumpets...
make a joyful noise
before the Lord, the King."**
Psalm 98:6

This section con-
sists of 2 to 5 <u>trum-
pets</u>, 2 to 8
French
horns,
2 to 4 trom-
bones, and 1 tuba.

(4) The Percussion Section

**"Praise him [the Lord]
upon the loud cymbals:
praise him upon the
high sounding cymbals."**
Psalm 150:5

This includes 2 or more
timpani, or kettle drums, <u>cymbals</u>,
gong, snare drum, xylophone,
triangle, bass drum, and bells.

(5) Miscellaneous Instruments

**"Praise the Lord
with harp...."**
Psalm 33:2

These can include the <u>harp</u>,
organ, <u>piano</u>, <u>harpsichord</u>, and saxo-
phones.

Symphony orchestras are **lovely** to listen to and can be a great blessing. But only if they play music that is a <u>form of worship to God</u>, a <u>praise to Him</u>, in <u>perfect order</u>, <u>sweet and calm</u>, <u>full and rich</u>, <u>melodious</u>, and <u>harmonious</u>. You will not want to listen to any orchestras that does not follow the principles of heaven!

Reinforce

1. Go through your house (or outside) and find items with strings, wood that is shaped like an woodwind instrument, and metal that is the color of brass. (Example: shoe strings; walking stick; the frame on a mirror.)

2. Take a walk outside and find things in nature that remind you of each principle of heavenly music. (For example: the smell of a rose is sweet like principle 4.)

Remind

1. As you tie your shoe strings you can think of the strings on a violin. Can your shoe strings make a sound like violin strings?

2. Sabbath morning when your mother tells you to get ready to go and to be in the car by 8:30, be quick about it. And when you are on time to church and hear the hymns being sung, remember how each member of the symphony orchestra must be on time to produce beautiful music.

Read the article on the next page entitled, "God's Natural Orchestra."

God's Great Natural Orchestra and Chorus

Did you know that God has an orchestra in nature? In fact, in the very beginning Adam and Eve would join in song with some of the members of this symphony of sound. "The happy birds flitted about them without fear; and as their glad songs ascended to the praise of their Creator, Adam and Eve united with them in thanksgiving to the Father and the Son."*

"How did man gain his knowledge of how to devise [invent]?—From the Lord, by studying the formation and habits of different animals. Every animal is a lesson book, and from the use they make of their bodies and the weapons provided them, men have learned to make apparatus [such as instruments, tools] for every kind of work [or you could say, music]."** Perhaps Adam and Eve studied the different animals and their sounds to discover more about music. Boy Jesus "studied the life the life of man." "Apart from the unholy ways of the world, He gathered stores of scientific knowledge from nature."*** Jesus **loved** to study God's second book.

> **"Great improvement can be made in singing. Some think that the louder they sing, the more music they make: but noise is not music. Good singing is like the music of the birds— subdued and melodious."**
> *II Sermons and Talks* 246

Patriarchs and Prophets 50   **1 Bible Commentary* 1089   ****The Desire of Ages* 70

Before the Flood men had great intellects far beyond what men have today. They studied the animals and learned many interesting things about the art of music. After the Flood "the Lord trusted His wisdom more sparingly to men."* We too could learn a great deal about music by again studying God's creatures for Job 12:7-8 says: *"But ask now the beasts, and they shall teach thee; and the fowls of the air, and they shall tell thee: Or speak to the earth, and it shall teach thee; and the fishes of the sea shall declare unto thee."* People did not create the theory of music they only discovered its rules. **What could these creatures have to tell us about music?**

Let us now look at some of God's magnificent musicians in nature. **Did you know God's songsters are composers?** One of the most prolific composers in nature is the little lark! It makes up to 4,000 variations on its songs in one day. It sings in C-major which is the most natural representation of nature's songs.

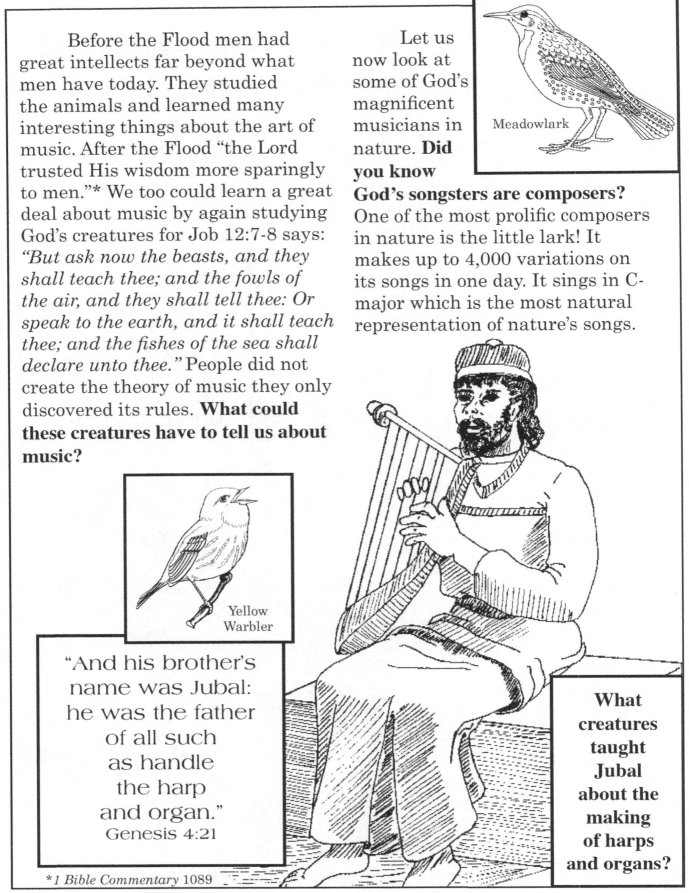

Meadowlark

Yellow Warbler

"And his brother's name was Jubal: he was the father of all such as handle the harp and organ."
Genesis 4:21

What creatures taught Jubal about the making of harps and organs?

*1 Bible Commentary 1089

In the animal kingdom, the great deep has always been represented as being silent. **Did you know that the ocean, especially the deep sea, is filled with sound?** "There is whistling and grunting, rattling and snoring and ringing, sawing and creaking and electronic noises, snapping and snipping and crackling, the beating of bass drums and tom-toms and tambourines, [as well as sounds which show there is sin now in the world like] screaming and howling, groaning and moaning. And the fish producing these sounds have names like drums and croakers, spot snappers, parrotfish, catfish, white grunts, trunkfishes, tunas wrasses, black gobies, snapping shrimps, sea robins."*

Of all the sounds in the ocean the humpback whale is the most unique. It sings the longest song in the animal kingdom and some of the most complex and beautiful songs known to nature. **What is in a Humpback Whale song?** A phrase is made up of several repeated elements. Identical phrases are strung together to form a theme and several themes form a whole song of chirps, moans, cries, snores, yups, moans, and ooos of sound.

Exactly how they produce the sounds is not fully understood. They have no vocal cords, yet the sounds produced cover a wider frequency range than that of any other whale.

The most basic unit of the song is a single sound or "element." They may be long groans, low moans, roaring sounds, trills, and chirps, and are arranged into simple repeating patterns usually with two to four different sound types. These short strings of sounds are repeated several times and are known as "phrases."

A collection of identical phrases is known as a "theme" and the singer moves from one theme to the next without pausing. There may be up to seven or eight themes in a song, and these are sung in a specific order, from first to last. After the last theme the singer surfaces to breathe, then sounds again to start the song from the first theme. Each song (full set of themes) may last from around six to fifteen minutes and sometimes even longer.

The song itself is an amazing phenomenon. It is highly structured, with at any one time, all the males in the population singing the

*The World of Sound 76 **Ibid 78*

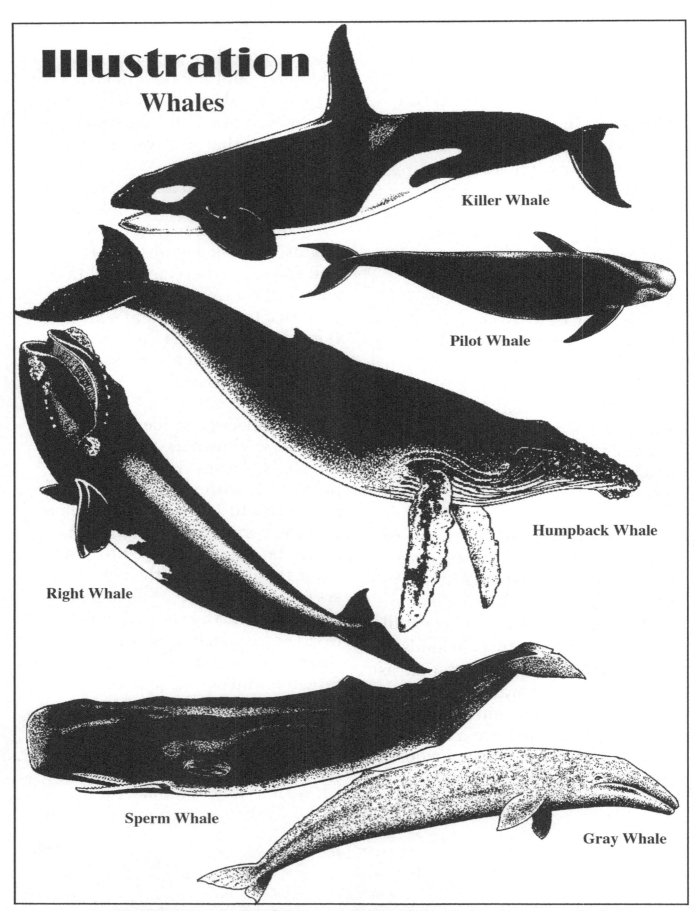

Illustration
Whales

Killer Whale

Pilot Whale

Humpback Whale

Right Whale

Sperm Whale

Gray Whale

same song using the same sounds arranged in the same pattern. Over time, however, this pattern changes, but all the singers make the same changes to their songs. After a few years the song may be quite different, but on any given day, all of the male humpbacks in an area will be singing the exact same tune. The year's song will start off where last years' song ended, which provides evidence for an amazing memory capacity. Some whales may carry a note a bit longer than another whale, but the structure and components [parts] are the same. This phenomenon extends beyond the whales in the area like Hawaii and includes the whales that are part of this population that migrate to Japan and to Baja. Scientists are not sure how this is possible, as it insinuates long distance communication, over thousands of miles. One possible explanation is the theory that humpbacks visit different breeding grounds in one season. The song could be passed on by these travelers but it is not known for sure.

Singers are usually lone animals staying in one spot. They sing about 50-60 feet (15-18 meters) below the surface. They point their heads downwards and their tails upwards. The males space themselves about 1/2 mile (8 kilometers) away from other singers, which may imply territoriality. The theme reverberates a hundred or more miles (kilometers) through the sea. Since the first scientist described and identified the whale song in 1979 in Hawaii, the song has never repeated itself, and is continually being written. The whale song is also unique to each population so the North Atlantic whales sing a completely different song than the whales around Hawaii.

Humpback whales are noted for their complex and beautiful songs.

Blue Whale

Identify the Humpback Whale on the previous page.

What else in nature sings? "It was also assumed until recently that plants, like sea creatures, were silent. After all, they grow soundlessly. No form of life is more noiseless than theirs. It was found, however, that there are sounds also in the realm of vegetation. In Israel, Great Britain, and the United States, photo-acoustic [having to do with the senses or the organs of hearing] spectroscopy [the examination and analysis of spectra] has been used to make the sound of a rose audible at the moment when the bud bursts into blossom: it is an organ-like droning, reminiscent [suggestive] of the sounds of a Bach toccata or Messiaen's *Ascension* or organ—in other words, reminiscent of what in traditional organ music is perceived as a 'spread' succession of chords."*

In other research it has been shown that even a simple corn stalk has a sound. Imagine thousands of stalks growing side by side in a field, each with its own unique sound—a waving symphony of sounds. The human ear cannot hear it as it takes special equipment to perceive such music.

"Research has also shown that plants in a meadow, field, or forest will wither if their vibrations—in other words, their sounds—relate disharmonically [without harmony] to other plants in the vicinity [nearby area—*"His enemy came and sowed tares among the wheat"* Matthew 13:25]. Flower lovers have always known that certain kinds of plants do not do well in close proximity [nearness] to certain other kinds, even though they may favor the same types of soil and climate. We now know the reason for this phenomenon [a fact]. The plants do not go together because their vibrations do not harmonize, because their sounds do not fit together, because they are in disharmony—or, in harmonic terms: because their sounds do not 'swing' together in low whole numbers.

"It is no wonder, then, that plants can also 'hear' and differentiate between various kinds of music."*

> **A simple corn stalk has a sound. Imagine thousands of stalks growing side by side in a field, each with its own unique sound—a waving symphony of sounds.**

The World of Sound 78

Reinforce

Take a few of the same kind (such as petunias) of hearty, healthy plants and place each one in separate rooms, then play same kind (one room—music with rock principles, another classical, another hymns, etc.) of music for each of them continuously. Of course, each would receive the same amount of water, sunlight, and care. See how plants that hear music that does not follow God's laws grow. Notice the ones that hear the music that follows the rules of heaven. Keep accurate record.

Petunias

Many creatures sound like musical instruments. **What are some of them?** One good example of this is the male hermit thrush who begins its song with a clean note. It then sings in ascending and descending tones that sound like flutes playing in clear tones.

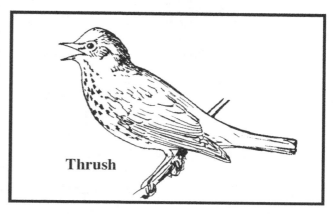

Thrush

The bellbirds make the sound of chimes. People have described their sound as a slow tolling of a bell which is heard up to many miles (kilometers). Others say they sound like drawn out chimes and even some say it sounds like a black-smith's hammer on an anvil. It probably depends upon the species as to the exact sound it makes.

Storks clatter their bills to make various sounds, while albatrosses have a vocal honk, but often clatter their bills also as two birds whack them together. Feathers of the hummingbird's tail make a whistling noise as the bird arcs or dives. Then there are the

Marabou Stork

Laysan Albatross

Hermit Hummingbird

Downy Woodpecker

Goldeneye

Common Snipe

sounds are actually produced by air rushing through the special stiff, tapered outer wing feathers. Even the common snipe sings with its tail. On rapidly vibrating wings, it gives its flight song high above the marsh. It circles around and around, periodically dashing downward and producing an eerie ventriloquistic [making the noise seem to come from another place] sound, as the air rushes past the unique rigid outer tail feathers. All of these are such amazing musicians in nature's orchestra!

woodpeckers which made drumming sounds on trees whereas the male ruffed grouse produces a low drumming sound by beating his wings rapidly together. A mourning dove leaves its perch with loudly whistling wings, and a duck called the goldeneye produces such a loud sweet sound with its wings that hunters call it the "whistler." The woodcock sings with its wings. It has an elaborate flight song and a good part of the twittering musical

Birds fit so well in God's great natural chorus. Unlike humans, which have a complex larynx with its cartilage and vocal cords situated at the upper end of the trachea or windpipe, birds have a simple larnyx. Instead, the voice box of birds, called the syrinx, is situated at the lower end of the windpipe where the two bronchial tubes branch.

Illustration
Bird Sounds

Esophagus

Trachea

Lung

The air sacs are connected to the lungs.

Barred owls hoot in baritone while the great horned owl hoot is bass. The screech owl has a quavering series of plaintive whistles which usually descends the scale. The barn owl has several explosive steamlike hisses and at times gives a call which sounds as though the bird were slamming on rusty brakes. The well-named saw-whet owl sings with a steady series of evenly spaced mechanical, repetitious whistles resembling the sound made by running a file over the teeth of a saw.

In addition to lungs, birds have a complex and remarkable system of air sacs which virtually fill the body cavity. The degree of development of these air sacs varies considerably from species to species. It is believed that birds with extensive uninterrupted songs such as winter wrens, purple finches, and highly trained canaries utilize the reserve air supply stored in these air sacs. It seems they sing without hardly stopping to take a breath.

Nearly all birds have a voice and use it to call or sing.

Barn Owl

Screech Owl

Barred Owl

Great Horned Own

Some birds such as the starlings and mockingbirds imitate the various sounds in their environment. You could say, they can sing any part as needed in the choir. Scientists have analyzed the songs of mockingbirds and some have listed over three dozen fairly perfect imitations of other birds given by a single mockingbird.

Careful research has revealed that some birds begin singing at a surprisingly early age. At first the performances tend to be decidedly poor, but by imitation and repetition the birds gradually develop and perfect their full characteristic song. This is certainly an encouragement for children to start singing very young.

Starling

Mockingbird

Reinforce

1. Run a file over the teeth of a hand saw to hear the sound made by some birds.

2. Listen to a recording of a variety of bird songs.

3. Go for an early morning bird walk and listen to the birds singing.

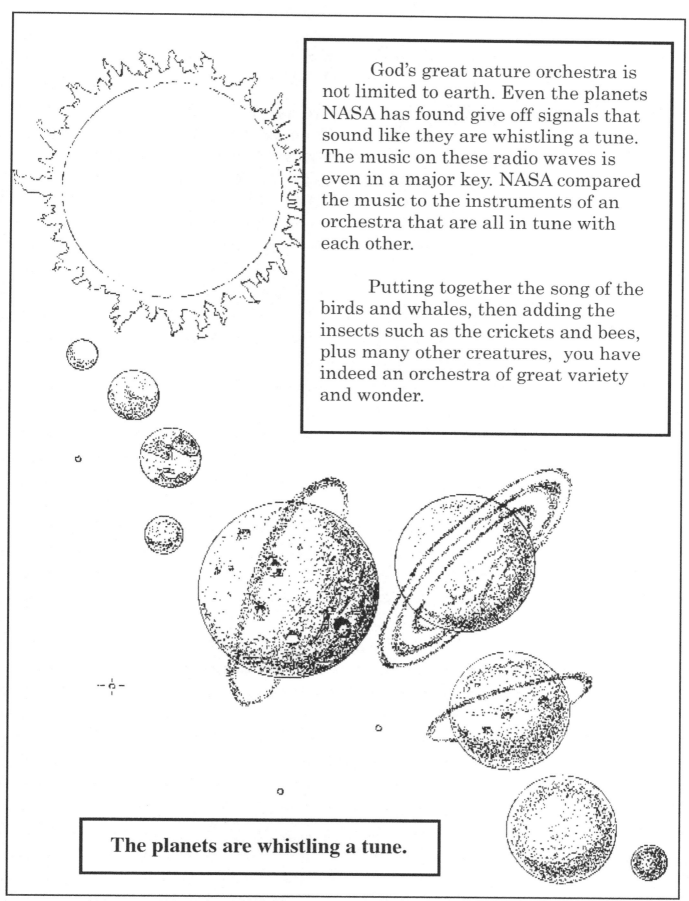

God's great nature orchestra is not limited to earth. Even the planets NASA has found give off signals that sound like they are whistling a tune. The music on these radio waves is even in a major key. NASA compared the music to the instruments of an orchestra that are all in tune with each other.

Putting together the song of the birds and whales, then adding the insects such as the crickets and bees, plus many other creatures, you have indeed an orchestra of great variety and wonder.

The planets are whistling a tune.

Review
Place I - II - III

"And David and all the house of Israel played before the Lord on all manner of instruments made of fir wood, even on harps, and on psalteries, and on timbrels, and on cornets, and on cymbals."
2 Samuel 6:5

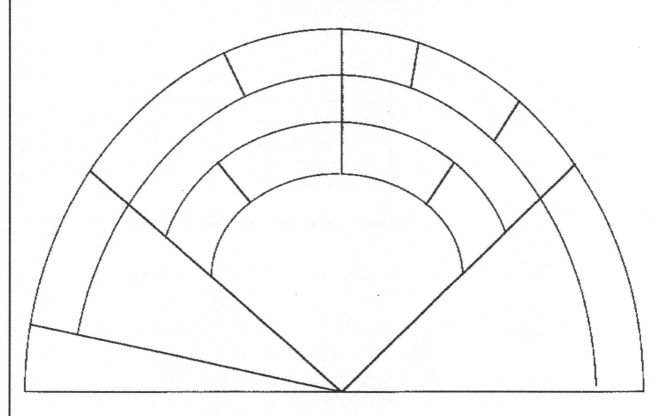

Place the correct instrument's number in the places on the orchestra layout above.

1. 1st Violins
2. Harp
3. Percussion
4. Trumpets
5. French Horns
6. Trombones
7. Tubas
8. Bass Violins
9. 2nd Violins
10. Clarinets
11. Bassoons
    Contra Bassoons
12. Piccolos
13. Flutes
14. Oboes
15. English Horns
16. Cellos
17. Violas
18. Conductor
19. Piano

Remainder

**"And I saw...
them that had
gotten the victory...
stand on the sea of glass,
having the harps of God.
And they sing
the song of Moses...
and the song
of the Lamb...."
Revelation 15:2-3**

Music that glorifies God by following the 7 principles of heavenly music is **lovely** in its sound; and it is out of **love** for man that God gave the gift of music. When we experience the music of true **love** in our hearts, it is because <u>God is with us</u>. Then the angels can join in our songs of praise because our souls are in harmony with the symphony of heaven. And one day soon we shall stand on that sea of glass and behold our God face to face. We shall at last be able to <u>hear and sing</u> with the heavenly choir!

O Love of God

O **love** of God, how strong and true!
Eternal, and yet ever new;
Uncomprehended and unbought,
Beyond all knowledge and all thought.

O wide-embracing, wondrous **love**!
We read Thee in the sky above;
We read Thee in the earth below,
In seas that swell, and streams that flow.

We read Thee best in Him who came
To bear for us the cross of shame;
Sent by the Father from on high,
Our life to live, our death to die.

We read Thy power to bless and save,
E'en in the darkness of the grave;
Still more in resurrection light
We read the fullness of Thy might.

O **love** of God, our shield and stay
Through all the perils of our way!
Eternal **love**, in Thee we rest,
Forever safe, forever blest.

—Horatius Bonar

**"O come, let us sing unto the Lord:
let us make a joyful noise
to the rock of our salvation.
"Let us come before his presence
with thanksgiving, and make a joyful noise
unto him with psalms."
Psalm 95:1-2**

More Love to Thee

The story behind the words.

As tears flowed down Elizabeth Prentiss' checks she asked her minister husband, "Why should this happen to us, of all people?"

Her husband responded sympathetically, "Maybe we should ask ourselves why a thing like this should not happen to us? Are we better than any of the other families who have lost loved ones in this epidemic? Does God owe us a special favor that He does not owe any other family? Or does He play favorites with anyone?"

Dropping her face in her hands, Mrs. Prentiss wept for a long time. Her thoughts traveled over all she had done up to that time when death had come to claim her loved ones. She was born in Portland, Maine to a devout clergyman. Early in life she displayed unusual literary talent. At the young age of sixteen she contributed regularly to one of the nation's leading magazines. At age twenty-seven she became the bride of Pas-tor George L. Prentiss and moved to New York City.

Tragedy struck after eleven years of marriage in 1856 and took away from the family circle the precious loved ones. Mrs. Prentiss was almost inconsolable for weeks. Church members were so kind and did all they could to help.

One evening after returning home from the cemetery Mrs. Prentiss said, "George, 'The night is dark and I am far from home.' What are we to do now? Just sit silently, passively by while our home is broken up, our lives wrecked, our hopes shattered, our dreams dissolved?"

Lovingly Pastor Prentiss replied, "This is our opportunity to show forth in our lives that which we have been preaching and teaching and believing together for so many years." He went on to tell of God's **love** for us, especially in trials. "Suffering," said he, "is used for God's glory."

Later that evening, Pastor Prentiss went out to make several pastoral calls. Mrs. Prentiss sat in the living room and thumbed through the Bible. She read several selections then looked through the hymnal. From the hymns she was seeking for light and consolation which reflected sorrows as well as triumphs of other Christians in similar experiences. As she read she meditated and prayed. Then she began to write down some lines of her own.

> More **love** to Thee, O Christ,
>   More **love** to Thee;
> Hear Thou the prayer I make,
>   On bended knee.
> This is my earnest plea,
>   More **love** O Christ, to Thee;
> More **love** to Thee.

That same evening Mrs. Prentiss completed four stanzas, but her husband did not see them until thirteen years later.

When we have more **love** for Christ our music shall be in harmony with heaven.

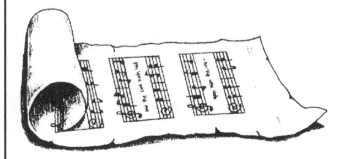

Reflect

"Thousands of sweet tones have come from eight little notes. This is wonderful; but there is something still more wonderful: millions of good deeds have come from four little letters. What word do they spell?

See Romans 13:10.

—Unknown

Reinforce

Sing the hymn, "More <u>Love</u> to Thee."

More Love to Thee

1. Is there music in heaven?

Revelation 5:8-9 – *"And...the four beasts and four and twenty elders fell down before the Lamb, having every one of them harps...And they sung a new song, saying, Thou art worthy..."*

2. Should God's people play or listen to music that is not following heavenly principles?

John 17:16 – *"They* [His disciples] *are not of the world, even as I am not of the world."*

Romans 12:2 – *"And be not conformed to this world: but be ye transformed by the renewing of your mind, that ye may prove what is that good, and acceptable, and perfect, will of God."*

3. Will the redeemed play music in heaven?

Revelation 15:2-3 – *"And I saw...them that had gotten the victory...stand on the sea of glass, having the harps of God. And they sing the song of Moses...and the song of the Lamb...."*

4. Where will the redeemed learn to play in harmony with heaven?

Isaiah 1:17 – *"Learn to do well."*

Psalm 25:8 – *"Good and upright is the Lord: therefore will He teach sinners in the way."*

The Principles of Heavenly Music

1. Form of Worship

Revelation 14:2-3 – *"...I heard the voice of harpers harping with their harps: And they sung as it were a new song <u>before the throne</u>...."*

2. Praise To God

Luke 2:13-14 – *"And suddenly there was with the angel a multitude of the heavenly host <u>praising</u> God, and saying, Glory to God in the highest, and on earth peace, good will toward men."*

3. Perfect Order

I Corinthians 14:33, 40 – *"For God is not the author of confusion...* [Therefore] *let <u>all</u> things be done decently and in order."*

4. Sweet and Calm

Psalm 119:103 – *"How <u>sweet</u> are thy words unto my taste! yea, <u>sweeter</u> than honey to my mouth!"*

Revelation 1:15 – *"...And his [Jesus'] voice as the sound of <u>many waters</u>."*

I Kings 19:12 – *"And after the earthquake a fire; but the LORD was not in the fire: and after the fire a <u>still</u> [calm] <u>small</u> [sweet-sounding] <u>voice.</u>"*

5. Full and Rich

Job 38:7 – *"...The morning stars sang together, and all the sons of God <u>shouted</u> for joy."*

6. Melodious

Isaiah 6:3 – *"Holy, holy, holy, is the Lord of hosts."*

Ephesians 5:19 – *"Speaking to yourselves in psalms and hymns and spiritual songs, singing and making melody in your heart to the Lord."*

7. Harmonious

II Chronicles 5:13 – *"...The trumpeters and singers were as one [harmony], to make one sound [harmony] to be heard in praising and thanking the Lord....."*

John 17:21 – *"That they all may be <u>one</u>; as thou, Father, art in me, and I in thee, that they also may be <u>one</u> in us...."*

Outline of School Program

Age	Grade	Program
Birth through Age 7	Babies Kindergarten and Pre-school	*Family Bible Lessons* (This includes: Bible, Science–Nature, and Character)
Age 8	First Grade	*Family Bible Lessons* (This includes: Bible, Science–Nature, and Character) + Language Program (*Writing and Spelling Road to Reading and Thinking* [WSRRT])
Age 9-14 or 15	Second through Eighth Grade	*The Desire of all Nations* (This includes: Health, Mathematics, Music, Science–Nature, History/Geography/Prophecy, Language, and Voice–Speech) + Continue using WSRRT
Ages 15 or 16-19	Ninth through Twelfth Grade	9 – *Cross and Its Shadow I** + Appropriate Academic Books 10 – *Cross and Its Shadow II** + Appropriate Academic Books 11 – *Daniel the Prophet** + Appropriate Academic Books 12 – *The Seer of Patmos** (Revelation) + Appropriate Academic Books *or you could continue using *The Desire of Ages*
Ages 20-25	College	Apprenticeship

Made in the USA
Las Vegas, NV
19 September 2021